Michael Dunn

The Penguin Guide to Real Draught Beer

Penguin Books

Penguin Books Ltd, Harmondsworth,
Middlesex, England
Penguin Books, 625 Madison Avenue,
New York, New York 10022, U.S.A.
Penguin Books Australia Ltd, Ringwood,
Victoria, Australia
Penguin Books Canada Ltd, 2801 John Street,
Markham, Ontario, Canada L3R 1B4
Penguin Books (N.Z.) Ltd, 182–190 Wairau Road,
Auckland 10, New Zealand

First published 1979

Made and printed in Great Britain by
C. Nicholls & Company Ltd,
The Philips Park Press, Manchester
Set in Intertype Times

Penguin Handbooks
Penguin Guide to Real Draught Beer

Mike Dunn was born and brought up in Leicester, and later took a first-class honours degree in geography from the University of Birmingham. He has subsequently been a research officer concerned with the problems of countryside planning, concentrating especially on landscape planning and the problems of housing and population movement in rural areas. He helped to found the Birmingham branch of the Campaign for Real Ale, later became its chairman, and was elected to the national executive of C A M R A in 1976, becoming particularly involved in producing proposals to curb, and ultimately reduce, monopoly power in the brewing industry. He is married and lives in Kings Norton.

For my wife, Chris

Contents

Preface and Acknowledgements

This book would never have been written had it not been for the growth of the half-dozen giant firms which have come to dominate the British brewing industry. Their policies of acquisition, rationalization and standardization have robbed the beer drinker of much of his heritage and denied him a large measure of choice. Such policies, too, have threatened the survival of real draught beer. But they have also provoked an angry reaction, of which this book is a part. Even two years ago this reaction might have seemed short-term, a mere hiccup in the big brewers' steady progress; now, however, it is clear that tradition, quality and choice in the world of beer have an exciting and long-term future.

Such a renaissance is not without its problems, however. New small breweries are springing up; established brewers are having to overturn their existing policies and produce new real draught beers. Inevitably, therefore, this guide will become progressively out-of-date, although within this constraint every effort has been made to ensure its accuracy.

Many individuals and organizations have assisted in the compilation of this guide, and I am grateful to all of them. I am indebted especially to the Campaign for Real Ale for giving permission for the original gravity figures in Chapter 5 to be quoted; to Wadworth & Co. Ltd for permission to use the diagram of the brewing process in Chapter 1; to Terry Hughes for converting my initial rough sketch into the diagram of beer in the cellar and at the bar; to Christopher Pope and Denis Holliday, of Eldridge, Pope & Co. Ltd, and

Martin Griffiths, of Penrhos Court, for valuable discussions; and to Chris Bruton for his comments on an early draft of the first chapter.

Amongst the many others who have been of real help, albeit sometimes unwittingly, I would like to thank Tim Amsden, John Bishopp, Barry Court, Andrew Cunningham, Peter Foy, James Lynch, Charles Marlow, Pat McCarthy, Kevin McKeown, Ian Mihell, Mike Nutt, Denis Palmer, Paul Pearson and Steve Ward.

Finally, though, I must place on record my gratitude to my wife, Chris, whose encouragement helped this book to reach fruition, and whose company in countless British pubs made the research so much more enjoyable.

Kings Norton, Birmingham
April 1978

1 Beer in the Brewery and at the Pub

Massive and far-reaching changes have been taking place in British pubs, and in the beer we drink inside them, over the last ten years or so. Two changes in particular threaten the character of both our pubs and our beer. Local brews, with their distinctive flavours, brewed especially for the varying tastes of different areas of the country, have gradually disappeared as local breweries have been bought up and closed down by a number of national brewery companies, which now dominate brewing in Britain. These companies, determined to create their own national identity, have not only gutted thousands of individual pubs and replaced them with stereotyped designs lacking individuality and atmosphere, but have also made every effort to tear the heart out of British beer. The big companies have tried to replace traditionally-brewed draught beer, served naturally, with keg and bright beers which are often weaker, usually more expensive, and which invariably lack the true taste and character of real draught beer. The result has been a drinkers' revolution, spearheaded by CAMRA, the Campaign for Real Ale, which may yet ensure the future of traditional draught beers, and force the brewers to take into account the wishes of their customers in deciding which beers to produce.

British beer, of course, is unique in the way in which it is brewed and served. Beer brewed from malted barley was part of the staple diet in Mesopotamia by about 3000 B.C. – indeed, it has been suggested that about two-fifths of the cereals produced at this time were used for brewing. Beer had been introduced to Britain before the Roman invasion, but it was not until the fifteenth century, with the introduction of hops from Flanders, that the beverage which modern drinkers would recognize as beer was first brewed in this country. Hops were introduced mainly as a preservative, and there was some resistance to their use: brews which contained hops were called 'beer', whereas the traditional name of 'ale' was reserved for the unhopped drink. Ale was usually stronger than beer, since this was the only way to make it keep. By the end of the eighteenth century, however, hops were almost always used in brewing and the words 'ale' and 'beer' came to be synonymous.

Although the main focus of this book is upon real draught beer, this introductory chapter surveys all the different types of beer available in Britain today, from the processes involved in brewing them, through serving them in the pub, to the choices facing the beer drinker in deciding what to drink. For the fact remains that despite the disappearance of so many local brews over the years, the British drinker has a considerable range of beers to choose from: over 300 traditional draught beers, a similar number of pressurized bright and keg beers, and well over a thousand bottled beers. The choice between different beers is not always an easy one, since questions of flavour, strength, price and so on all have to be taken into consideration. Selective advertising on a massive scale by the larger brewers, chiefly aimed at selling their nationally available brands (which may compare badly in terms of value for money, or flavour, but which have a carefully constructed image), is another factor clouding the issue. The basic issues, however, concern the way in which the beer is made – the quality of the ingredients and the way they are used – and the way in which it is kept and served at the pub.

Beer made from the traditional raw materials of malted barley, hops, water and perhaps brewing sugars, together with yeast, brewed by traditional methods to produce a living beer still fermenting in casks in the pub cellar, and brought to the glass by simply turning a tap in the barrel itself, or by drawing it up by means of a pump, can conveniently be described as real draught beer – 'real ale' according to CAMRA. Modern developments in the brewing industry, usually aimed at cutting costs or producing a standardized beer, have often departed from these ideals. Alternatives to malted barley or to whole hop cones have been introduced, sometimes to the detriment of the resulting beer; methods of filtering beer, making it easier to handle, but removing much of the flavour, are widespread; the increasing use of carbon dioxide pressure to force beer out of the container in the pub cellar has been widely condemned.

After comparing the types of beer available, therefore, the rest of this book concentrates on real draught beer, undoubtedly the outstanding example of the brewer's art, considering in turn its history, the emergence of threats to its continued existence, the qualities likely to ensure its future and, perhaps most important, the breweries which continue to produce real draught beer. First, however, there is a description of the brewing process, both for the traditional beers and for their modern processed substitutes, and a look at the publican's part in presenting the drinker with his choice of different types of beer, each of which is then described in terms of flavour, strength and value for money.

Certainly there are some brewers who would argue that the drinker has no need to know anything about the ingredients used in brewing his pint, or the way in which it is brewed, or how strong it is. Such an argument ignores the fact that different raw materials and different methods produce beers of different quality. Why else would John Young, chairman of Young's, the independent brewers based at Wandsworth, state that 'our definition of beer is that it is brewed from malted barley and hops, and we have no use for wheat, flour, rice or potato starch, all much cheaper materials'? Fortunately, the Food Standards Committee of the Ministry of Agriculture, Fisheries and Food, reporting on beer in 1977, felt that the consumer had the right to be given 'adequate information regarding the existing range of beers and any new or modified products'. That view would no doubt be widely supported by beer drinkers in search of a fair deal; in these terms, a comparison of traditional and modern brewing methods is extremely revealing.

Inside the Brewery: How Traditional Draught Beer is Brewed

Typically, the brewer's tasks begin at about six o'clock in the morning, and have been largely completed by the early afternoon. By then the raw materials used in the brewing process have been converted into a liquid which will, over the next five or six days, produce 'green beer', which is then matured for a further period until it is ready for drinking. Many traditional breweries were constructed on the tower principle, as shown in the diagram, so that the early stages of the process take place at the top of the brewery and the brew travels downwards by gravity, before being pumped up again after it leaves the hopback. The diagram also shows that traditional draught and keg beers are both brewed in the same general way, until the beginning of the conditioning process. The description of the progress of a typical beer through all the processes in a traditional brewery is therefore common to almost all British beers. The story of brewing, however, begins long before, with the cultivation and preparation of malting barley and hops, and so the first stage to be described is that of malting.

Malting – the conversion of barley grains into fermentable malt, an ideal material for brewing – was often carried out by the brewery companies themselves, although this practice has become less common for a number of reasons. Wadworth's, for example, had its own maltings next to the brewery in Devizes until 1964, but then built a new wine and spirits store on the site of the maltings; Donnington Brewery malted its own barley, grown on the farmland around the brewery, until the 1960s, but rising production costs and the small amounts involved forced it to stop doing so, and to buy its supplies from maltsters in Cirencester instead. But a number of companies still own active maltings – Banks's and Hanson's (Wolverhampton & Dudley Breweries), for instance, obtains malted barley from its own premises in Lichfield, and Paine's of St Neots runs a sizable business as maltsters in addition to its brewing activities.

Inside a traditional maltings, the barley is 'steeped' or immersed in water, and then spread on the floor of the maltings to a depth of up to two feet, so that it begins to germinate, and small green shoots and roots appear. The barley is constantly shovelled over by a maltster, whose job it is to gauge the time at which the germination process needs to be stopped by kilning the barley, or heating it to a temperature of between 80°C. and 110°C. Barley kilned at the lower temperature produces pale ale malt; higher temperatures produce mild ale malt, and a further roasting at an even higher temperature results in chocolate and black malts, mainly used in producing stouts. At this point the malt is stored ready for delivery in sacks to the brewery's malt store, where it is kept until needed for brewing.

Milling, the first process in the brewery itself, involves the preparation of the malt for brewing. First the malt is screened to remove impurities and to grade the corns of malt by size. Then it is milled to produce a coarse powder known as grist. The extent to which the malt is milled has to be very carefully controlled, and often different grades of corns are cracked open by different rollers. Ideally the grain is crushed into small particles, but the husk is kept intact; if the malt

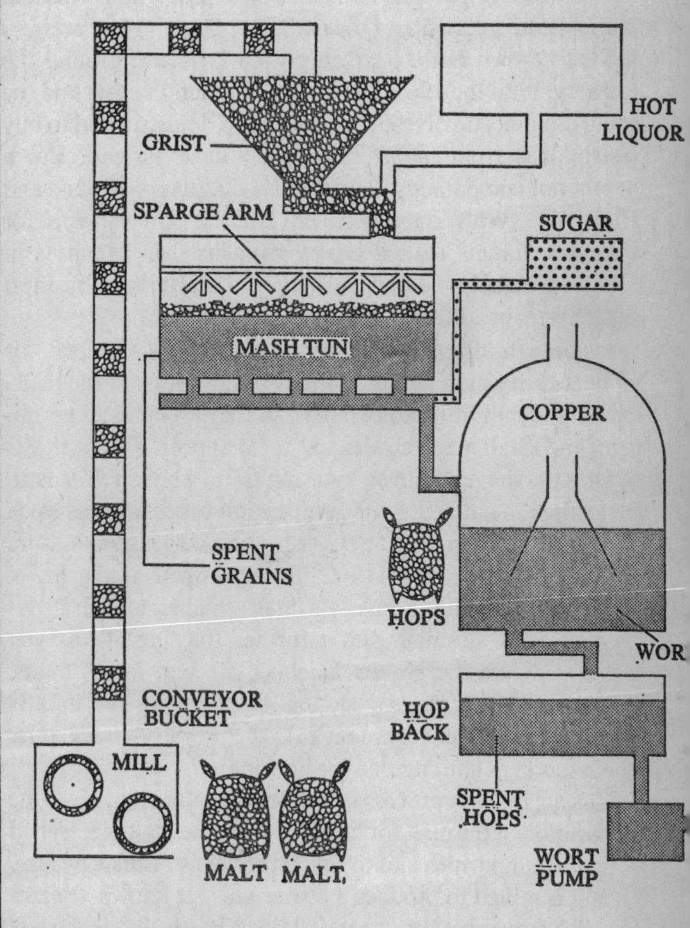
HOW REAL DRAUGHT BEER IS BREWED
GRIST
HOT LIQUOR
SPARGE ARM
SUGAR
MASH TUN
COPPER
SPENT GRAINS
HOPS
WOR
CONVEYOR BUCKET
HOP BACK
MILL
SPENT HOPS
WORT PUMP
MALT
MALT

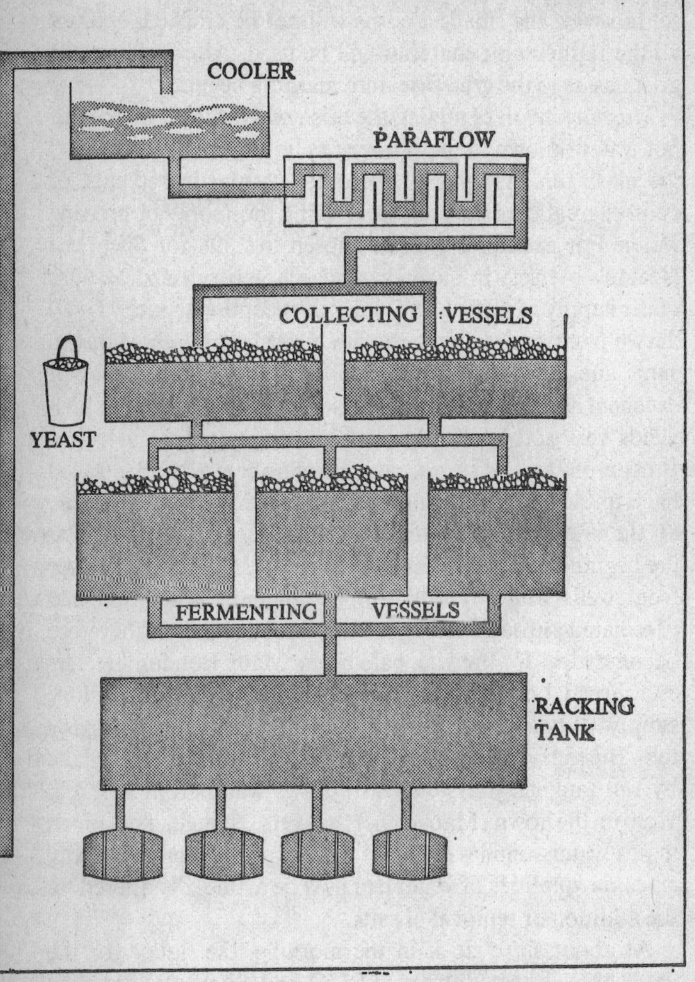
COOLER
PARAFLOW
COLLECTING VESSELS
YEAST
FERMENTING VESSELS
RACKING TANK

is milled too finely, the rollers may cake up, and the later process of mashing may be impaired. But if the rollers are set too wide the smallest corns will not be cracked, and not all the fermentable material will be used. After milling, the grist passes to the grist case until mashing begins.

Mashing involves mixing the grist, or powdered malt, with hot water (known in the brewery as liquor) in a vessel called the mash tun. As with all the other natural ingredients, of course, great care is taken in selecting the supply of brewing water. For example, the site chosen in 1698 for Shepherd Neame's brewery in Faversham was largely selected because of the supply of water: and water of exceptional purity is still drawn from an artesian well with a 200-foot borehole on the same site. King & Barnes of Horsham, another brewer of excellent and distinctive beers, also has an artesian well which yields very soft water ideal for brewing. And the secret of Burton-on-Trent's success as a brewing centre can be traced back to the existence of deposits of gypsum under the town; all the breweries in the town – and there were twenty-six at the beginning of the twentieth century – drew brewing water from wells which tapped supplies of pure water that had percolated through the beds of gypsum and had therefore become ideal for brewing pale beers. Many London brewers established breweries in Burton in the nineteenth century simply to take advantage of the water, and one company took Burton well-water to its brewery in the north of England by rail tankers. Marston's still draws water from its Field Well in the town. Many other brewers, though, find piped mains water supplies equally suitable for brewing, especially since the qualities of water can now be artificially altered by the addition or removal of salts.

At about six o'clock in the morning, the liquor for the day's brew is heated to about 65 °C. and allowed to flow into the mash tun to mix with the grist in carefully calculated proportions, so that the hot liquor can slowly extract the sugars which contribute strength to the finished product. This conversion process is largely completed within an hour; and, after a further period during which the mash is allowed to stand, the resulting sweet extract, now known as 'wort', is drawn off by opening plates in the bottom of the mash tun. The spent grains, however, are retained on the false bottom of the mash tun, and sparged – sprayed with hot liquor – to remove any remaining sugars. The grains can then be removed from the tun and sold to farmers as a useful source of cattle feed. The sweet wort, on the other hand, flows into the copper to be boiled with the hops.

Boiling the wort in the presence of the hops fulfils a number of functions: it sterilizes the liquid, allows essential oils and flavour to be extracted from the hops, and removes undesirable materials extracted during the mashing process. The length of the boil varies from one to two hours, during which time hops are gradually added; normally, some are held back until the last few minutes, so that their aroma is carried through into the final product instead of evaporating during the boil. The boiling process takes place in the copper, a vessel which has been traditionally made of that material, but which is nowadays sometimes stainless steel. Originally coppers were merely open vats heated by wood or coal fires at their base; but, as the scale of production increased, more efficient vessels were introduced which were fitted with a chimney to allow excess steam to escape from the brewery, and which were heated by steam passing around coils in the lower part of the copper.

Although hops are now recognized as a universal ingredient of British beer, they were not introduced to this country until after 1400, and they did not become a common crop in parts of England until the end of the seventeenth century. Now, however, hop gardens (or hop yards), fields criss-crossed by systems of tall poles and taut wires to prevent the crop from trailing along the ground, are a familiar sight in parts of Kent, Hampshire, and Hereford & Worcester. Just as familiar are the oast-houses where the hops are spread to a depth of six inches or so before being dried and compressed into six-foot hessian 'pockets', large sacks in which they may be kept for up to a year before use.

A number of brewers also own hop farms (Whitbread at Beltring in Kent and Guinness, near Hawkhurst in the same county, are two examples), and Shepherd Neame's hop farm, Queen Court at Ospringe, two miles from their Faversham brewery, produces all the hops they need – varieties such as Early Bird, Eastwell Goldings, Tutsham and Cobbs. The traditional English varieties such as Goldings and Fuggles are in fact gradually being replaced to a large extent by varieties with greater bittering power and more resistance to disease.

Back in the brewery, the brewer may add brewing sugars while the wort is boiling with the hops in the copper. A number of breweries still produce beer from malt and hops only, but the practice of adding sugar to increase the fermentable material in the brew, which was permitted for the first time as late as the mid-nineteenth century, has become widespread – Bass Worthington and Hook Norton, almost at the extremes of the scale of production, are both amongst those who add sugars to the hopped wort. When boiling has been completed, the contents of the copper are allowed to flow into the hopback. The spent hops settle onto the false bottom of the hopback (just like the grains on the bottom of the mash tun) and act as a filter through which the hopped wort passes before being pumped up to the cooler at the top of the brewery. The spent hops can then be removed and sold for use in the manufacture of fertilizers.

Cooling, which is necessary to prepare the wort for fermentation, is a process which has been considerably improved over the years. There are, however, still a number of breweries where the hot hopped wort is simply pumped into a shallow open trough and allowed to cool down gradually. King & Barnes and Hook Norton are two breweries which use open coolers, though both use them in conjunction with more modern cooling equipment. Quite apart from the time taken for the beer to cool in open troughs, the beer is exposed to bacterial infection from the air, so that the introduction of modern, compact heat exchangers, known as paraflow refrigerators, which reduce the temperature of the wort to about 15°C. by pumping it against a counter-current of cold water separated from the beer by thin plates, has been very beneficial. Whilst the beer is being cooled in this way it may also be aerated (in other words, its level of oxygen may be increased) in order to stimulate the yeast into rapid action when it is added.

At Wadworth's in Devizes, though not in all breweries, the hopped wort is run from the cooler into collecting vessels, where yeast is added to it and the excise officer is able to measure the quantity and gravity (strength) of the wort in order to calculate the amount of duty payable on the brew (the strength of beer is discussed in more detail in the final section of this chapter). After about sixteen hours Wadworth's drops the wort from collecting vessels into the fermenting vessels – a process which causes aeration and thereby increases yeast activity. Other brewers, however, run the hopped wort from the cooler straight into fermenting vessels, have the brew 'dipped' for excise purposes, and then pitch the yeast.

Fermentation, the conversion of the sugars in the wort into alcohol and natural carbon dioxide by the action of the yeast, is perhaps the most critical part of the brewing process, and is certainly the stage which requires most care. Yeast, a single-celled fungus, is 'pitched' or poured into the wort as a slurry (occasionally it may be added in a powdered form), and within twenty-four hours it produces a spectacular thick head or crust of yeast on the surface of the wort. A typical strain of yeast will multiply five times during fermentation, so that it becomes necessary to remove the yeast head by skimming – either manually, using paddles, or by a variety of automatic methods, Paine's of St Neots, for instance, using a parachute device, a large funnel which draws in the excess yeast. Some of the yeast which is removed in this way is later used to pitch further brews, but a good deal is surplus to the brewery's requirements and forms a further by-product of the brewing process, since it is pressed and then sold to yeast extract manufacturers. The fermentation progresses rapidly for up to three days, although it gradually slows down as the fermentable sugars are converted and the specific gravity of the wort falls. The beer normally matures in the fermenters for about a further three days – until six or seven days have passed since it was brewed – and it is then cooled so that most of the yeast suspended in the liquid settles out, and the 'green beer' is ready for the conditioning process.

Traditionally the fermenting vessel was an open rectangular vessel, originally constructed from wood (often oak) and later from slate – Samuel Smith's of Tadcaster, a company very proud of its 'traditional' image, still uses slate Yorkshire squares. Later still, copper became the most common material for fermenters, and recently stainless steel, which is easier to clean and maintain, has become popular. Many different types of fermenting vessels have been used, although most are now obsolete, and the 'Burton Union' system is the only one which survives as an alternative. Bateman's of Wainfleet, for example, replaced its system of carriage casks in 1953. In this system, a primitive forerunner of the Burton Union method, wort was run into large casks which were positioned over open troughs, and yeast and beer which overflowed from the vigorous fermentation in the casks was returned to the casks every three hours day and night. Losses of wort during fermentation totalled eight per cent, much higher than is normal, and this proved to be an excellent motive for Bateman's to install a stainless-steel fermenting room.

In the Burton Union system, which was developed in the nineteenth century because it was found to be ideal for use with the yeast which was commonly used in the town, the fermenting wort is run after a day or so in conventional square fermenting vessels into the Union Room, where it lies in huge oak casks called unions, each of which holds 144 gallons. The activity of the yeast as it ferments in the unions causes wort and yeast to rise through swan-necked pipes into the barm trough, which runs above and between two long rows of unions. The yeast sediments in this trough, while the wort eventually runs back into the unions. The yeast therefore continually circulates through the beer, giving it a characteristic flavour as a result. Nowadays union sets are used at only two breweries, both in Burton: at Bass Worthington, where the immense Union Room is an awe-inspiring sight, and at Marston's, where it is said that the unions are retained despite the high costs of cleaning and maintenance because of the higher quality of the beer they produce.

A more modern alternative to the open square type of fermenting vessel is the conical fermenter, a completely enclosed tall cylindrical tank with a conical base. In this system the yeast sediments during fermentation and is removed from the conical base. Many modern breweries, including Thwaites of Blackburn and Shepherd Neame, have installed these fermenters, which save space and can be extremely efficient in that the time taken for fermentation can be reduced to as little as two days. Excellent traditional beer can be produced in this way as long as 'batch' fermentation – the procedure described above – is practised, and the fermenters are emptied and cleaned between each brew; but 'continuous' fermentation, a process which can seriously affect the character of the brew (as described later in this chapter) can also be carried out in conical fermenters. Whatever the method of batch fermentation, however – open squares, Burton Unions or conical fermenters – the green beer which has been produced now needs a period of conditioning or maturation before it is ready to leave the brewery.

Conditioning is a process which varies from brewery to brewery, depending on whether the beer is to be matured wholly in casks, or partly in conditioning tanks before being transferred to casks. Until the beginning of the twentieth century, the green beer was invariably 'racked' or allowed to flow via a racking back (a vessel designed to control the flow) from the fermenting vessels direct into casks of various sizes. The casks could be made of either wood or metal – the material makes little or no difference to the beer – and the size, normally from 4½ to 54 gallons, would be tailored to the amount of trade of individual pubs. Although this method is now less common, it is still in use at a good number of smaller breweries. When the cask is full, a bung is fitted and a shive placed in the hole midway down the side of the cask. The casks are then laid on their sides in the brewery cellar and left to mature for a number of days – the exact length of time depending mostly on the strength of the beer, since strong beers will normally take longer to mature. The maturing beer still contains a small quantity of yeast carried forward from the fermenting vessel, and this continues to promote a slow fermentation, producing the natural carbon dioxide which is necessary to obtain liveliness when the beer is served. This process of conditioning beer wholly in the cask has, however, now been largely replaced: in many breweries green beer from the fermenting vessels is now run into maturation tanks and held there for some days. This is partly to allow more of the sediment to be extracted before the beer leaves the brewery, and partly to cut down on the length of time it needs to be kept in the pub cellar before being served.

In the cask or in the maturation tank, finings may be added in order to clear the remaining yeast cells and other solids from the beer. Finings consist of a material obtained from the swim bladders of certain fish, and about two pints per barrel (36 gallons) of beer are sufficient to act on the yeast and cause it to sediment at the bottom of the barrel. Finings may be poured manually into the cask or injected through a stainless-steel needle, as at Eldridge Pope in Dorchester. Other additions to the beer at this stage may include priming sugars, which are added in order to promote a further slight fermentation which will increase the strength of the beer marginally, but more importantly will help to remove some of the flavours associated with raw beer and will assist in producing the correct level of natural carbon dioxide in the beer. Some brewers, such as King & Barnes, add primings only to their darker beers – draught mild and old ale in their case – whilst others treat all of their beers in this way.

Immediately before the beer is racked into the casks it may also be 'dry hopped': that is, a small quantity of hops will be added to impart a pleasant aroma when the beer is served. Whole hops are used less now than they were in the past, largely because they were difficult to remove from empty casks, and so hop pellets, formed by compressing powdered hops, are often added instead. In some cases, indeed, hop oils, in which the bittering substances of the hops are highly concentrated, are added instead of dry hopping. Usually only the finest hops are used in dry hopping: Bass Worthington uses two ounces of Kentish Goldings per barrel to add an extra aroma to the palate of its beer.

So far the description of the traditional brewing process has concentrated entirely on the steps which are followed in the production of draught beer. There are also, however, a small number of bottled beers still produced which are naturally conditioned in the bottle, and which should therefore be mentioned here. The production process for these beers is exactly the same as that for real draught beer as far as the end of fermentation; the beer may then be run into conditioning tanks, or it may be allowed to run straight into bottles. Originally all bottled beers were handled in this way, and the small amount of yeast remaining in the beer was allowed to promote a secondary fermentation to assist in the maturation process and give the beer its sparkle. Once the yeast had exhausted the supply of fermentable sugars in the bottle, it formed a sediment on the bottom, and the beer could be poured carefully in order to leave the sediment in the bottle. Not all bottles cleared completely, however. The time and care needed to pour the beer was also a problem, so new bottling methods were introduced. Now only a handful of bottled beers, such as Guinness, Worthington's White Shield and Courage Russian Imperial Stout, are naturally conditioned; they are all described in Chapter 5.

Whether in cask or bottle, the beer is now ready to leave the brewery on its journey to the pub cellar. Real draught beer has taken something like two to three weeks to travel from the brewhouse, through the fermentation hall and the conditioning and racking processes, to the point where it is loaded onto the dray, or delivery vehicle – which was traditionally horse-drawn (and which still may be on short journeys from breweries like Wadworth's or Young's) but is now much more likely to be a lorry or even an articulated truck.

The method of brewing is strikingly simple, and the end product one which is widely and increasingly acclaimed – yet the larger breweries have spent vast sums of money over the past two decades in attempting, above all for reasons of convenience and profit, to force the drinking public (which has shown no signs of asking for change to accept drastic changes in the nature of British beer. Before looking at beer in the pub, therefore, it is necessary to look at the reasons for the brewers' actions, and to describe the modern developments in brewing, many of which threaten the existence of real draught beer.

Modern Methods: Polluting the Pint?

Changes in the basic method of brewing have been brought about partly by advances in scientific understanding, but much more commonly as a response to economic factors (hence the use of inferior ingredients) or problems in the pub – bright beer, for example, was the brewers' answer to licensees who could not be bothered to look after traditional beer properly. Some of these changes, such as the introduction of conical fermenters, have been mentioned already, since they have merely made the traditional methods more efficient or subject to greater control. Many changes, however, have either threatened to alter the basic character of British beer, or have led to the introduction of a completely different type of beer, and for this reason they are dealt with separately in this section.

Almost all the stages in the brewing process have been tampered with to some extent. British brewers are particularly free to do this, unlike their Bavarian colleagues (and those on the Isle of Man) who are restricted by law in what they can put into the brew. New developments in malting have replaced the need for 'old-fashioned' malting floors; different cereals have been introduced to take the place of some or all of the malted barley; hop powders and hop extracts are widely used; continuous fermentation systems have been installed in a few cases. Nevertheless, as Peter Mathias says in *The Brewing Industry in England 1800–1930*, 'an eighteenth-century brewer would be quite at home in a present day brewery provided he did not visit the sections of the plant devoted to processing after fermentation.' Modern methods of conditioning, maturing and packaging beer have created sterile, bulk-conditioned beers which, pushed from the pub cellar to the bar by carbon-dioxide pressure, are fizzy, gassy and devoid of distinctive flavour – hence the need for extensive advertising to sell them. The following account attempts to explain the differences between traditional beers and their modern processed counterparts, as well as describing the actual processes involved.

Malted barley is the original and traditional source of fermentable sugars for brewing, yet there has been an increasing tendency on the part of some brewers to use cheaper substitutes to make up some of the fermentable material. Indeed, as early as the middle of the nineteenth century, brewers sought to use other cereals, although this was mainly an attempt to avoid the tax which was levied on malt at that time. Naturally, some of the smaller brewers, arguably those producing the most distinctive beers, have resisted the temptation – John Young's feeling on the matter has been quoted already, and Belhaven Brewery of Dunbar is another firm that uses 100 per cent malted barley in the grist (in fact their main trade was in malt until the early 1970s, although this side of the business has now been phased out completely).

Nationally, however, the average grist lowered into the mash tun consists of 77 per cent malt, so that almost a quarter of the fermentable material is composed of such products as flaked maize or maize grits, wheat flour, barley flakes, rice or even potato flour. Since relatively few beers are brewed at present from less than 70 per cent malted barley, it is clear that most draught beer now contains a fair proportion of malt adjuncts. This is not automatically a problem – the addition of small amounts of brewing flour, for example, may help the beer which is eventually produced to retain a creamy head in the glass – but the addition of significant quantities of unmalted cereals unquestionably affects the final product considerably in terms of flavour and quality. The use of semi-malted, or torrefied, barley tends especially to mask the normal malty tang of beer with a sweet and insipid taste. Malt extracts – concentrated syrups extracted from malted barley – have a similar effect on flavour, and would be better confined to home brewing, where mash tuns are not normally available. The extraction and concentration processes involved in producing malt extract tend to remove subtle flavouring materials along with the water, and therefore extract beers tend to be thin, bland and devoid of strong flavour.

One stage further on in the brewing process is copper boiling, where whole hop flowers were traditionally boiled with the sweet wort. But both the type of hops used, and the way in which they are prepared for the copper, have been subject to major changes in the more 'progressive' breweries. Traditional varieties such as Goldings and Fuggles, whilst providing excellent hops for brewing purposes, are prone to disease; and, in the process of developing hops which are disease-resistant, growers have also produced varieties with greater bittering qualities (that is, with a higher alpha-acid content). This may be more convenient and efficient for the brewers, but obviously the new products affect beer flavour and aroma, not always beneficially. Not only has the raw material altered, but so has the method of incorporating it in the brew: whole hops are being replaced by powdered hops, which are more convenient and take up less storage space, or hop extracts, which are far more efficient and, if specially treated, may be added *after* fermentation. During the conditioning process the practice of dry hopping may be replaced by that of adding hop oils to give the beer its characteristic aroma. The result is that beers may be produced entirely from extracts and oils, without ever coming into contact with whole hops.

By now, 'modern' beers may be far removed from their natural predecessors, yet even further adulteration is awaiting them during fermentation. The source of this extra pollution is silicone antifoam, which is added to the wort during fermentation to reduce the head of yeast which builds up, and which thereby allows a greater amount of wort to be fermented in the fermenting vessel. Again, the driving force behind this innovation is that of economics – in this case the more efficient use of the fermenting vessels during peak production periods – rather than improvements in the beer itself. And, although brewers claim that the silicone is removed from the beer before it leaves the brewery, there is evidence to suggest that residual amounts are still present at the pub in beer which has been produced in this way.

Much more of a threat to the existence of traditional draught beer, perhaps, is posed by the development of the technique known as continuous fermentation. The most common type of continuous fermenter consists of a vertical tower, up to thirty feet high and about six feet in diameter. A very high concentration of yeast is maintained in the conical base of the fermenter, and wort passes through this yeast and rises up the tower, fermenting rapidly as a result of its contact with much more yeast than in a traditional open square fermenting vessel. At the top of the tower the beer is separated from the yeast, which sediments back into the conical base. There are obvious advantages in this system: the fermentation is much more rapid than usual, taking only about ten to twelve hours compared with as much as seven days in a conventional vessel, and because the process is continuous no cleaning of the fermenter is involved. There is consequently an obvious saving of manpower in the brewery.

Despite these advantages, however, the use of continuous fermentation methods has not become widespread, although its benefits were vigorously promoted in the early 1960s and a number of experimental schemes were set up. One reason is that the development of the conical fermenter, which also speeds up the process, but which is capable of turning out acceptable traditional beer, has been rapid. Continuous fermentation, on the other hand, produces beer which is 'totally out of character and lacks the subtleties and flavour of beer produced by the conventional method', according to Stephen Foster in *What's Brewing*, the CAMRA newspaper. A further problem surrounds the yeast in the base of the tower: it must be kept completely free from bacterial infection, or else the bacteria may multiply faster than the yeast, with disastrous results both for the brew and the fermenter, which must be emptied, cleaned and sterilized before fresh yeast and wort can be pumped in. Most of the big brewers have experimented with continuous fermenters, but only Bass, at its new keg factory at Runcorn, and a handful of others, have installed and retained towers at production scale. Even if the method is adopted more widely, it seems obvious that most smaller firms will not have the finance, the technical know-how or, most important of all, the inclination to install towers. As the Food Standards Committee states, 'batch production still remains the most flexible, efficient and economical method of producing beer.' Given that existing methods can produce outstanding beers economically, it seems ridiculous that brewers should even try to change their ways.

With the exception of continuous fermentation, however, this description of new and generally unwelcome developments has concentrated so far on the question of *ingredients* rather than on the *processes* by which the beer is produced. This is largely because all beer is mashed, boiled, cooled and fermented in similar ways (with exceptions such as lager, which is fermented much more slowly at a lower temperature). After fermentation, however, real draught beer and the newer processed varieties are treated separately. The careful maturation of real draught beer has already been described; the conditioning of processed beers involves new processes, of which the most important are chilling, filtration and pasteurization.

Sometimes beer destined for this modern form of conditioning passes from the fermentation vessel into maturation tanks, where it may be held at around 15°C. for several days. It is then chilled through contact with a coolant, and the beer temperature is lowered to about freezing point. At this temperature most of the residual solids, including yeast, form a sediment, and the beer is then ready for filtration. As with most other departures from traditional methods, the introduction of filtration is the result of economic forces, which have persuaded brewers to devise quicker methods of maturing and clearing the beer. Certainly there has been little consideration of the effects upon quality; the result is that not just the flavour, but the character of beer is completely changed when filtration takes place. Essentially the difference is between real draught beer, a living product in which the fermentation continues in the pub cellar, and filtered beer, which is sterile (all the living yeast organisms having been removed) and which needs added carbon dioxide in order to recreate the 'lively' appearance of draught beer.

During filtration beer is pumped through a cloth filter which has been coated with a thick pad of powder called kieselguhr, derived from very small fossilized skeletons. As the beer passes through the filter pad the remaining yeast and other solids are trapped, and the resultant liquid is 'bright' beer (also known as brewery-conditioned or chilled and filtered beer). Bright beer is extremely clear, hence the name, and contains virtually no sediment, but is also requires an increase in the level of carbon dioxide to restore an appearance of life to the beer. Filtered beer may then be pumped direct into the packaging plant, or it may be further treated by pasteurization.

The object of pasteurization is to make sure that any remaining life in the beer (perhaps still there because of inefficient filtration) is destroyed by heat, thereby ensuring that no haze or flavour problems develop before the beer is sold. However, it is generally accepted that the process can also give beer a rather stale taste, known as 'pasteurization tang', and so brewers have tried alternative methods such as chemical sterilization. Beer destined for kegging is pasteurized by being passed through a heat exchanger in which it is held at about 65°C. for several minutes before being cooled. Bottled and canned beers, on the other hand, are packaged first and then sent on a conveyor belt through a pasteurizer unit, in which they are sprayed with hot water for about fifteen or twenty minutes. Pasteurization, as well as being a process which has detrimental effects on both the flavour and the character of beer, is also extremely expensive process to install and run; but the alternative of chemically sterilized beer is even more dubious, to the extent that it has been suggested that chemical additives of this sort should be completely banned.

Bright beer, whether pasteurized or not, now passes to the packaging plant, either to be kegged or 'casked', or to be kept in large holding tanks ready to be pumped into road tankers and delivered to pubs with large cellar tanks. Kegs are sealed containers which are pressurized with carbon dioxide, and beers stored in them are always filtered and usually pasteurized. More carbon dioxide is also needed in the pub cellar, to force beer from the keg to the bar. Beer from cellar tanks is usually carbonated to a lesser degree, especially where the beer is stored in a plastic bag inside the tank, so that the gas and the beer it is pushing out do not actually come into contact. But the beer is still carbonated and therefore fizzy, and the carbon dioxide masks any real flavour which has survived chilling and filtering. As Stephen Foster says, we have seen the creation of beers 'whose flavour is harshened by malt extract, hop extract, silicone antifoam, industrial enzymes, head promoting chemicals, haze preventers and the processes of filtration and pasteurization' – all because of apparent economies (which, oddly enough, don't result in keg and bright beers being cheaper than their real draught counterparts: quite the opposite, in fact) and the problems caused by a few poor licensees. Arthur Willis, secretary of the Yorkshire Clubs Brewery (regrettably, taken over and closed down by the Northern Clubs Federation Brewery in 1975), summed up the purely negative factors behind the rise of bright beers when he said that 'our draught beer trade has been declining over the years because keg and tank are easier to keep.' No reference there to bright beers being *better* than the five excellent draught beers which Yorkshire Clubs brewed – indeed, Willis himself prefers real beer 'because it's got a fuller flavour'.

Reference has already been made to the few bottled beers which are still naturally conditioned – that is, which contain yeast in the bottle and therefore undergo a secondary fermentation. All bottled beers, of course, were originally produced in this way, until the advent of pasteurization led to the production of stable, sterile beers with more consistent keeping qualities and hence a more predictable shelf life. This stabilized beer, since it is free of yeast, also has no problems with hazy or cloudy appearance in the glass. Bottling nowadays comprises a number of operations: the empty bottles are cleaned and sterilized, then filled with beer, and conveyed to a machine where crown corks are forced on to the top to seal the contents. The bottles then pass to the pasteurizing unit, before being labelled and loaded into crates ready for delivery to the pub. Most bottled beers are chilled, filtered, pasteurized and artificially carbonated, and suffer from the disadvantages of all these processes.

So far, then, the production of real draught beer has been described, together with more 'modern' techniques – involving either substitute ingredients, new additives designed to improve the process, or new methods of production – and the difference between traditional cask-conditioned beer, a living substance which is still fermenting in the cask in the pub cellar, and bright (or brewery-conditioned) beer (including all keg and lager beers) has been emphasized. Either or both of these types of beer may be available at any individual pub, but the next section of this chapter concentrates on real draught beer and the way in which the publican needs to look after it.

Real Draught Beer in the Pub

Well over half of Britain's pubs receive deliveries of beer which has left the brewery as traditional cask-conditioned ale. The tragedy is that a natural, traditional product is then ruined in thousands of these pubs, because although the first test – the way in which it has been brewed – has been passed, the second and third vital stages in the art of producing a traditional pint have further pitfalls. These stages, as indicated in the diagram, involve looking after the beer carefully as it matures in the cask, and then serving the beer in good condition. But some licensees use carbon dioxide to get cask-conditioned beer to the bar or simply to store such beer badly in the cellar. Again, this masks the true flavour of the beer, but it makes the licensee's job easier by reducing the skill needed for the job to the bare minimum.

What, then, is the art of the licensee in dealing with real draught beer? Initially, beer delivered from the brewery has to be stillaged; that is to say, the casks have to be placed in the position they will occupy while the secondary fermentation occurs and the residual solids (such as the yeast and the hop flowers used in dry hopping) are deposited on the bottom of the cask by the action of the finings. The casks cannot be moved again until all the beer has been drawn out – otherwise the sediment will be disturbed and 'cloudy' beer will be served. When the casks have been set up, either in the pub cellar or (in the case of smaller pubs with no

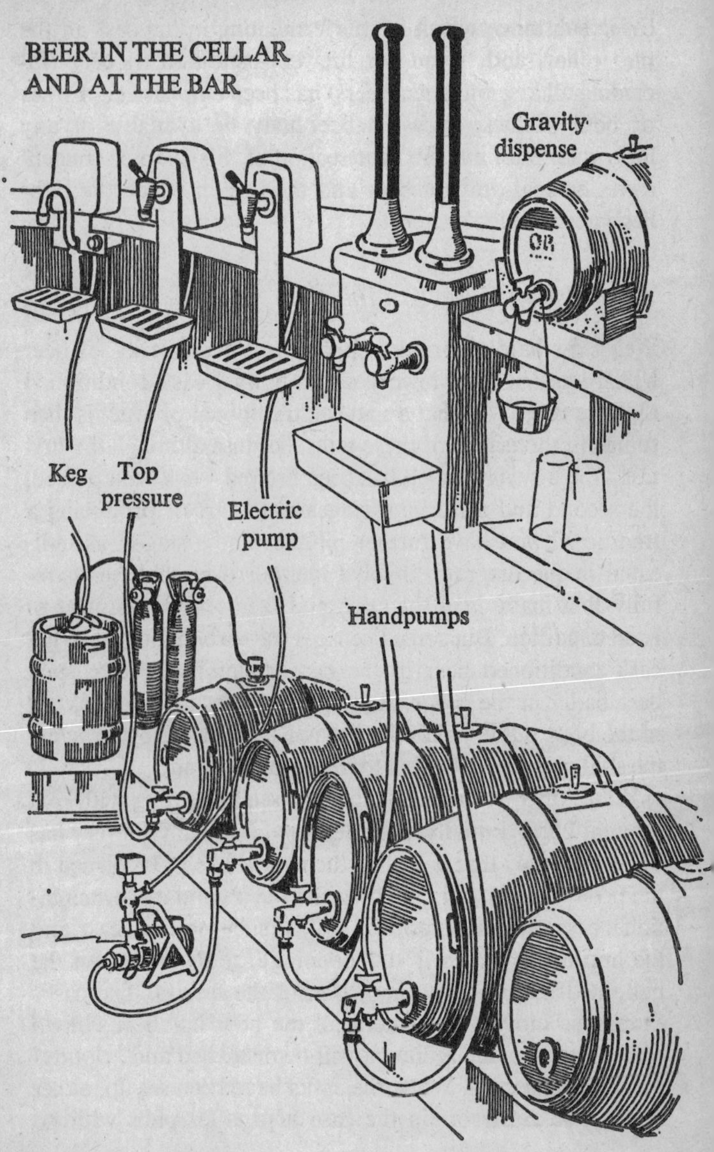
BEER IN THE CELLAR
AND AT THE BAR
Gravity
dispense
Keg
Top
pressure
Electric
pump
Handpumps

cellar facilities) behind the bar itself, and held in position on the stillion with wooden chocks, a spile peg is knocked through the shive midway down the cask. The spile peg, which is porous, assists the secondary fermentation by allowing excess natural carbon dioxide to escape. Normally a soft spile – which allows a lot of gas to escape – is used first, when the contents of the cask are fermenting vigorously, and it is replaced by a hard spile when the activity in the cask dies down somewhat. The hard spile lets less carbon dioxide through, and therefore ensures that enough is left in the cask to stop the beer going flat.

Different beers vary considerably in the time taken for the finings to deposit the sediment and clear the beer, although generally stronger beers take longer, and for these up to forty-eight hours or so may be required. The ale is then ready to be served, although the flavour of the beer may still vary slightly as a very slow secondary fermentation continues, and some experienced licenses refuse to broach casks until they have been in the cellar for seven days or even longer. Before starting to serve from the cask the last job is to knock a tap through the bung in the end of the cask, and to connect the tap to a length of tubing if the beer is to be pumped up to the bar. The cask will now have to be emptied within two or three days, because air will empty the cask to replace the beer which is drawn out, and this will eventually result in the flavour of the beer becoming unpleasantly stale. A good licensee, however, will be able to judge the most suitable size of casks for the trade he has, and since casks range from hogsheads (54 gallons) through barrels (36 gallons), kilderkins (18 gallons) and firkins (9 gallons) to pins (4½ gallons) he should have no difficulty in avoiding problems.

One crucial factor affecting beer in the pub is that of temperature, and this is why most pubs have cellars where the temperature does not vary much from the ideal of about 12·5°C, or air-conditioned rooms kept at that temperature.

Variations from this temperature may affect the secondary fermentation or make it difficult for the sediment to settle out completely, leading to cloudy beer. Certainly beer which is too cold lacks the full flavour which is associated with real draught beer, whereas beer served too warm is usually flat and insipid. Casks which are stillaged on the bar, or on racks behind the bar, are obviously especially prone to these difficulties, particularly during the height of summer. Hop sacks or cloths soaked in cold water may be draped over the casks to cool them, but this method is not always successful, and so some breweries have developed other ways of keeping beer cool. Wadworth's have in the past used cooling jackets filled with cold water, which circulates continuously around the outside of the cask, but they have now introduced a newer system using cooling probes which are fitted through the shive, so that the coolant in the probe can act more directly on the beer.

There are three universally recognized methods of serving real draught beer in its natural condition. The simplest of these is by gravity, that is by turning a tap in the cask and letting the beer run out into the glass. Many people feel that where it is practical this is the best method, since it avoids using pipes and other apparatus which can affect the taste of the beer unless they are kept spotlessly clean. Beer served in this way, however, has a flat appearance, since it lacks the creamy, textured head created by the action of pumping beer through a narrow opening. Gravity dispense tends to be confined these days to smaller country pubs, where the casks are stored behind the bar, although in some pubs beer is still carried from the cellar in jugs or glasses.

By far the commonest method of delivering traditional draught beer to the glass is by beer engine – either by a manual pump, more usually known as a handpump, or by electric pump. The sight of working handpumps on the bar is almost a guarantee of real beer (although some pubs belonging to certain brewers retain handpumps on the bar counter whilst dispensing bright beer from pressure taps below the counter). Certainly such a sight would be cited by most people as one of the central features of a traditional English pub. The invention of the manual beer engine has been credited to Joseph Bramah, whose other inventions included the hydraulic press and an improved water closet. The beer-pump device he patented in 1797 was rather more complicated than the present-day version, but simpler designs were soon in use, and within ten years handpumps were a common feature of the public house. The basic method has remained almost unaltered: the beer engine, below the bar counter, is a simple suction pump, which is normally designed so that a single pull on the handle displaces half a pint of beer from the cask through the pipes and into the glass. The nozzles, or sparklers, in the spout of the handpump are usually screwed tight in the north of England, where a foaming creamy head is normally regarded as a necessary part of the pint, and left much looser in the south, where drinkers are accustomed to beer with a flatter appearance (it is no coincidence that gravity dispense is also much more common in the south).

Handpumps are probably commonest in the south of England, where some breweries such as Shepherd Neame and Young's use them almost exclusively, but in the north of England, and in some parts of the Midlands, electric pumps are the usual method of dispense for real draught beer. The principle is exactly the same as that involved in manual pulls, since every time the barman operates a mechanism on the bar an electric motor situated near the casks in the cellar is switched on to provide the power to draw beer from the casks to the bar. There are a number of different designs for taps which operate electric pumps, although the most familiar is probably that which incorporates a glass cylinder through which half a pint (or occasionally, as in some Ward's pubs around Sheffield, a pint) of beer is automatically metered each time the tap is operated. Simpler taps known as 'free flow' dispensers activate the electric motor and therefore supply beer for as long as the tap is held open. Occasionally a push button system is used to dispense metered half pints of traditional draught beer. The second and third types mentioned look very similar to systems used to serve bright beer by carbon-dioxide pressure, and in many cases the only way to find out which system is being used is to ask the barman or taste the beer. Since such a difference in taste is involved, there is a strong case to be made for compelling breweries to tell the drinker what kind of beer is being served. Most Mitchell's & Butler's pubs, in fact, use an identical free-flow system for both real draught beer and pressurized beer, even where both types of beer are sold in the same pub.

Gravity dispense and the various types of beer engine, despite the fundamental differences in their design and operation, perform the same job in getting the beer from the cask to the glass without interfering with the natural flavour and character of the beer. The same cannot be said for systems which use carbon-dioxide pressure; the verdict of the impartial Food Standards Committee, that 'we accept the point that a high carbon-dioxide content in beer is detectable on the palate', emphasizes this point. Carbon dioxide may be used at a relatively low level while the beer is being stored, to keep air away from the beer ('blanket pressure' or 'flooding pressure') or a higher level of carbon dioxide may be used to force beer out of the cask and up to the bar ('top pressure'). Either of these methods produces marked differences in the palate of the beer, although the detrimental effect may vary from very little in the case of blanket pressure on a full cask to totally disastrous where top-pressure carbon dioxide has been dissolved into the beer over a fairly lengthy period.

To sum up, real draught beer is an easily identifiable product which possesses a number of very real virtues, one or more of which is lacking in all processed beers; it is brewed from high quality ingredients, with a high proportion of malted barley in the grist, and real hops added to the copper; it is allowed to continue fermenting in the cask whilst it is stored in the pub cellar; and it is served by traditional methods. So far, though, real draught beer has been described as though there were only one kind available; yet the great strength of traditional beer is that there is still a tremendous choice of different beers with a wide variety of flavours. Most breweries produce at least two real draught beers, and some of the smaller ones brew as many as six. The next section, therefore, looks at the different kinds of beer available in British pubs.

A Guide to Choice, Strength and Value for Money

The choice of real draught beer likely to be encountered in British pubs is the result of two main factors: the *type* of raw materials used, and the *amount*. To deal with the second factor first, the amount of malt used per barrel determines the body of the resulting beer, and to a large extent its strength: the more malt (and therefore fermentable sugars) the stronger the beer, all other things being equal. The type of malt used, on the other hand, will affect flavour and colouring. The amount of hops and their type will affect the flavour and aroma of the beer – fewer hops, and usually those with less bittering power, such as Northern Brewer, are added to produce mild ales, whereas hops like Goldings and Progress are used to produce bitter.

The strength of beer, of course, is inextricably bound up with types of beer, and so it is necessary to explain the way in which strength is measured. Two methods are widely used – original gravity and alcohol content – though the former of these is generally regarded as more useful. A third method, degrees Plato, may become more widely used in the future; it is calculated in a similar way to the original gravity, and one degree Plato is equivalent to approximately 4.08 degrees of gravity (although the relationship is not linear). The original gravity of a beer is a measure of the amount of raw materials used in making the beer, expressed in relation to the quantity of water used. The original gravity of water is taken to be 1000, so that a beer with an original gravity of 1040 would comprise 40 parts fermentable material to 1000 parts water. The weakest beers brewed nowadays have an original gravity of about 1030, the average pint of bitter is around 1038, and few draught beers are brewed at above 1050, except for the strongest bitters and a few barley wines and strong ales. The alcohol content of beer is measured as a percentage by volume, and varies from between two and three per cent for the weaker beers to five per cent for strong bitters and up to ten per cent or so for barley wines. Neither of the measures gives any real indication of the quality of the beer, although original gravity does indicate the body of beer, so that a beer brewed at 1050 is likely to be heavier and fuller flavoured than one brewed at 1030, which may be relatively thin and bland. Some beers brewed at higher gravities, however, taste very sweet compared with lower gravity brews, which may have more desirable flavour characteristics. The final judgement is clearly that of the individual drinker.

So the strength of beer, whilst it is useful in judging value for money, as will be shown later, is of little use in considering the choice and quality of real draught beer. What are the types of beer available nowadays? The first point to stress is the vast range still available despite the demise of so many local brews. Although many of the larger brewers restrict themselves to only one or two beers, a number of the more enterprising independent companies provide a much greater choice. Wadworth's, for example, brew three bitters of varying strength as well as a rich, mellow strong ale called Old Timer; Taylor's of Keighley produce six different brews, including the excellent Landlord best bitter, two more bitters, two milds, and Ram Tam strong ale. Other breweries as different as Shepherd Neame, Robinson's and Morrell's brew between four and six real draught beers. The traditional staple diet of the British beer drinker, however, is mild and ordinary bitter, and hence mild ale is considered first.

Mild accounted for 42 per cent of the beer produced in Britain in 1959; it now accounts for little more than ten per cent, and the proportion is still falling. To a large extent this is one of the results of selective advertising on the part of the brewers, who have recognized the greater sales potential (and greater profit margins) of bitter and have therefore spent millions in promoting it. Yet the vast majority of brewers still make a mild, and eleven of them, seven in Lancashire and Greater Manchester, brew more than one. Indeed, Robinson's sells more mild than bitter, and Holt's and Oldham Brewery sell about the same of each. In the West Midlands, 70 per cent of Banks's and Hanson's draught production is mild ale. The converse of this is obviously that some of the other firms brew very small quantities indeed, and so it is not surprising that a number of brewers have discontinued production of mild in recent years. Whitbread, for instance, stopped brewing XX light mild at Tiverton in 1976, and there are fears for many more. Mild accounts for only two per cent of Ridley's draught beer production, for example, and since it cannot afford to be any less efficient than the bigger brewers mild may well be doomed to extinction.

The future of mild, then, is threatened, and indeed it has completely disappeared from some parts of the country, such as large areas of Dorset, where it used to be a popular drink.

Yet it can be a cheap and tasty alternative to bitter, brewed as it is from darker malts, and with fewer hops added to the copper. Incidentally, brown ale is often just the bottled version of mild. It is certainly true that the use of fewer, and occasionally inferior, ingredients can result in a sweet, bland-tasting beer of no real merit, but there are a number of outstanding mild ales still brewed. Among the dark milds Thwaites's best mild, brewed in Blackburn, is full of flavour, and Bateman's DM is an excellent drink with a high reputation. Fuller's Hock, too, is a pleasant low-gravity alternative to the strong beers which often dominate London's pubs, although it is not all that widely available. Probably the best light milds are brewed in the north-west of England: Robinson's best mild is an excellent example. Samuel Smith's 4X best ale was another fine light mild, with more flavour than a number of bitters of comparable colour and gravity, until the brewery decided to keg it all in 1977. In the West Midlands, traditionally a mild-drinking area, and an area where the popularity of mild ale has been maintained, Banks's mild, which is relatively strong but delicately flavoured, and Ansell's mild have large followings.

A stronger version of mild beer, and one which seems to be gaining ground, is *old ale*, so called because it is normally matured for a longer period than ordinary beers. Usually old ale is a fairly sweet, rich, dark beer with an original gravity of 1045 or so. Only one or two of the dozens of breweries controlled by the big brewers make an old ale, Wethered's Winter Royal, brewed at Marlow, being the outstanding example. Several of the independent brewers continue to produce them, however, often for the winter months only. Brakspear's XXXX old ale is a magnificent beer with a clean, traditional 'old' flavour, and other examples include Gale's Winter Brew, King & Barnes's old ale and Tolly Cobbold Old Strong. *Stock ale* is nowadays rarely found on draught; again the name refers to a beer which is brewed over a longer period so that it can be held in stock over a greater period of time. Normally stock ale is dark but well hopped and has a characteristic bitterness, as is the case with Shepherd Neame's stock ale. Gray's stock ale, brewed in Chelmsford, was a superb strong, full-bodied beer which, sadly, died with the brewery when Gray's were forced to sell the brewery site and cease brewing in order to meet death duties in 1974.

Real draught *bitter*, however, is very much alive and well, with many breweries reporting substantial increases in sales. Normally bitter is a pale golden brown in colour, although the range of colour varies from a yellowish hue (Theakston's, for example) to a dark reddish-brown in the case of Morland's best bitter or Charles Wells's bitter. The degree of bitterness varies considerably, too, with the amount and type of hops used, although usually bitter is generously hopped in the copper, and may also be dry hopped before it leaves the brewery. Another variation lies in the strength of the beer, and many brewers offer two or more bitter ales with different original gravities. In the south-west of England low-gravity bitters are quite common: Hall & Woodhouse's pale ale, with a gravity of 1031, is often known as boy's bitter, and Devenish, Eldridge Pope and Palmer's, the other surviving Dorset brewers, all also make a weak bitter. There are a number of outstanding medium-strength bitters available which combine a full flavour with a characteristically dry, well-hopped taste: Wadworth's IPA and King & Barnes's bitter spring to mind. Conversely, a number of the beers which have become widely available in the free trade have a sweeter, malty palate, and one or two hardly warrant the name of 'bitter' at all.

Stronger bitters are usually, though not always, sweeter than ordinary bitter, and they are certainly more expensive. There is a good deal of confusion surrounding the terms 'best bitter' and 'special bitter', since the 'best' or 'special' produced by one brewery may be weaker than the ordinary bitter produced by its neighbour. Pale ale, and especially India Pale Ale, are also used to describe draught beers, but again different breweries use the words to describe different types of bitter. Stronger bitters are brewed with an original gravity of around 1042 or more, and amongst the best known are Marston's Pedigree, draught Bass and Ruddle's County. The strongest bitter in the country is Fuller's ESB (1056). Regrettably, perhaps, many of the real draught beers which have been introduced recently, such as Paine's EG, Everard's Old Original or Ind Coope's Draught Burton Ale, have been brewed at these higher gravities, when the clear demand for traditional beer may well be more for a good ordinary bitter which could provide a full evening's drinking.

Bottled versions of these beers are normally called light ale and, in the case of stronger bitters, pale ale. India Pale Ale originally referred to a beer brewed by Bass for the East India Company, but is now used indiscriminately to denote a premium pale ale. Other names which have been used to describe bottled bitter are Family Ale and Dinner Ale (the latter of which was used by Melbourn's of Stamford for the bottled version of their excellent draught bitter until the firm ceased brewing in 1974). Export Ale tends to be used for a high-gravity pale ale. Worthington's White Shield, which is naturally conditioned in the bottle, is probably the supreme example of a strong pale ale.

Strong ales and *barley wines*, the final varieties of real draught beer in Britain, seem to be increasingly popular, and a number of new ales of this type have recently been introduced. Strong ales may be light or dark in colour, and either sweet or dry; their one common characteristic is strength. Arkell's Kingsdown Ale, for example, is brewed at 1060 and yet it is a fairly bitter beer, whilst Samuel Smith's Old Samson, brewed at the same gravity, was dark and fairly sweet. College Ale is a term which was formerly used to describe strong beers brewed in the colleges of the older universities; in fact the medieval brewhouse at Queen's College, Oxford, survived until after the Second World War. Morrell's College Ale is still brewed in Oxford, and is an excellent high-gravity brew. Barley wines are the strongest of the range of beers, and are normally sold only in nips – bottles containing one-third of a pint. A small number are also available on draught, including Robinson's Old Tom, a superb full-bodied ale which is not too sweet, Marston's Owd Roger (first brewed at the Royal Standard of England at Forty Green in Buckinghamshire, which still sells it) and Harvey's Elizabethan Ale, an extremely strong pale beer.

Stout is not available in Britain as a real draught beer, although bottled Guinness is a naturally conditioned dry stout with a unique bitter flavour; the so-called draught Guinness is a keg beer, although a mixture of nitrogen and carbon dioxide, rather than carbon dioxide alone, is used to pressurize it. Real draught Guinness is, however, still available in southern Ireland. So too, until recently, was a weaker version which was known as porter. This beer, first brewed in London in the 1720s, was originally called 'entire' but supposedly acquired its later name because of its popularity with porters and other manual labourers. Sweet stout in bottles (often called milk stout until the Trade Descriptions Act came into force) is widely available, but the only naturally conditioned stout apart from Guinness is Courage Russian Imperial Stout, an extremely strong and quite bitter beer first brewed in the eighteenth century, and matured in the bottle for at least two years.

Little need be said about keg bitter and mild. Frank Baillie, in *The Beer Drinker's Companion*, sums up the position in a sentence: 'Keg beers are consistent, easy to handle, always bright, gassy, have a long shelf life after tapping, generally have little flavour or character, and are more expensive than draught beers.' In other words, they are consistently mediocre. *Lager*, however, is a special case because of the extraordinary way in which the brewers have promoted a product which is exceptionally weak, brewed from second-rate materials in many cases, and brewed using methods which often bear no relation to those used on the continent. Carlsberg and Tuborg, for example, have original gravities of 1030, weaker than virtually all other beers in the country; Harp and Heineken are brewed at 1033 (compared with an original gravity of 1048 for the Dutch version of Heineken) – figures which are hardly consistent with the image of strength and flavour conveyed in advertising campaigns. And the methods used in brewing British lager are often totally unlike the continental methods, as we shall see. No wonder the *Financial Times* considered that 'those brewers who produce top-fermented beers they call lager have a rather strange product and one which often deserves the industry's term for such beer – bastard lager.' Yet in the twelve months to June 1976 £5,600,000 was spent by the major brewers alone on press and television advertising of lager – more than one-third of the total expenditure on advertising for all beers. The intention of the brewers is clearly to create a taste for weak, cold and insipid beers which bear little or no resemblance to true continental lagers and above all have very high profit margins.

Occasionally there are suggestions that the resurgence of interest in traditional English beers could be complemented by the production of a 'real' lager. This ignores the very basic differences between real draught beer and true lager. Lager is brewed from lager malt, the brewing water is subjected to a special liquor treatment, a bottom-fermenting lager yeast is essential, the decoction system of mashing is preferred by most brewers (instead of the single infusion mash characteristic of English ale production), the temperature of fermentation and storage is much lower than for traditional draught beers, and the length of storage is much longer – as long as ten weeks or more for some lagers on the continent. Because the lager must be fermented and stored at a low temperature, filtration is necessary to remove proteins and other solids which would otherwise be precipitated out of solution and cause the final product to be cloudy.

So-called real lager *could* be produced – but it would have to be brewed with a different yeast, at a higher temperature, and with a shorter storage period: in other words, it would not be a true lager at all. It is more realistic to accept that lager is a product which is completely different from real draught beer, and which therefore has no place in this book.

Even though we do not have real lager in Britain, excellent real draught beer is obtainable on the continent – there are, for example, the alt beers of Düsseldorf, the Belgian trappiste beers, and kölsch beers from Cologne – but these are top-fermented ales and not lagers.

So much for the range of beers available; what is also useful is a comparison of them in terms of value for money – strength and flavour measured against their price in the pub. To understand the reasons for the comparatively low strength of British beer nowadays, it is necessary to see how excise duty is levied on each brew. The amount of duty paid is in fact directly proportional to the strength of the brew. This has not always been the case – though the present system was first introduced in 1880 – and indeed it is not a universal method of collecting duty. In West Germany, for example, tax and duty is levied on a sliding scale, so that big brewers pay proportionately more than smaller firms (an excellent argument against mergers). In Britain a minimum rate of duty is levied on a beer with an original gravity of 1030, with an additional amount for each extra degree of gravity. About one-third of the price paid over the bar for a beer of average strength eventually finds its way to the government, either in excise duty or value-added tax.

Brewers have historically been extremely coy over publishing details of the original gravities of their beers. Occasionally they have suggested that a full declaration would result in drinkers seeking out the strongest beers purely on strength alone. More realistically, some of them have been afraid of declaring gravities because this would reveal two things: first, that almost all brewers have been systematically reducing the gravities of their beers in order to reduce the amount of duty payable (it goes without saying that there is no evidence that these savings have been passed on to the customer) and second, that some brewers give a good deal less value for money than others, in some cases actually charging more for a weaker beer which has cost them less, in terms of both duty and raw materials, to produce. Some independent analyses of original gravity have been carried out, and almost without exception they support these points. For example, Stephen Hargreaves, the Warwickshire county trading standards officer, tested a variety of beers in 1972 and concluded that 'quality and strength have declined while prices have risen dramatically.'

The *Sunday Mirror*, in a survey published in March 1971, disclosed some quite remarkable changes in original gravity in comparison with the same beers when they had been tested by *Which?* in 1960. Ansell's bitter, for example, had dropped from 1045 to 1039; Watney's Special from 1043 to 1038 (no wonder the Advertising Standards Authority banned the advertisement which claimed in 1975 that 'sometimes I think that everything keeps changing except the taste of this'); and Worthington E from 1042 to 1037. CAMRA followed this up with a survey in 1975, and was able to show some further dramatic reductions in gravity. The original gravity of Ansell's Bitter had now dropped even further, to 1037 – an astonishing fall of nearly 22 per cent in fifteen years. Charrington IPA, which remained almost stable at around 1044 between 1960 and 1971, had now fallen to 1039. And the much-acclaimed draught Bass had been reduced in gravity from 1043 to 1039 (though in 1976 it was boosted to 1044 to provide Bass Charrington with a much-needed product for the strong draught bitter market).

The tests carried out by CAMRA undoubtedly had the effect of drawing attention to the progressive weakening of British beer, and in one or two cases they clearly prompted individual brewers to do something about it. Devenish, for example, brewing in Weymouth and Redruth, increased the strength of its ordinary bitter by more than two degrees to 1032 in the summer of 1975 because, in the words of their marketing director, 'we don't want to be branded as the brewers of the weakest beer.' And their higher-gravity bitter was renamed and increased in gravity to 1042 a few months later. Finally, in 1976, the brewers' reluctance to disclose gravities was shattered by the decision of CAMRA to publish a complete list in their *Good Beer Guide*. 75 out of 119 breweries, including three of the Big Six companies, volunteered the information, given the inevitability of publication; independent analysts calculated the gravities of the remaining brewers' beers from samples collected for the purpose.

This full publication of information to which many observers felt drinkers were entitled – to quote from the Food Standards Committee report again, 'we also think that the consumer has the right to be told when a product he has come to know well changes significantly' – also opened the way for a comprehensive examination of the extent to which different brewers are giving drinkers value for money. Some steps in this direction had already been taken, although the results were conclusive only in showing that, as the *Sunday Mirror* put it after a further survey in 1972, 'it is hard to understand why (keg) beer is becoming so popular. It is more expensive than other draught beers and on the whole its original gravity and alcohol content were no higher than ordinary bitter. Perhaps it sells on fizz appeal?' Watney's Red, for example, costs an average of 14p for a gravity of

1037, and Younger's Tartan, the weakest of the keg bitters at 1036, sold for between 13p and 15p; most draught bitters cost only 13p and were stronger, and Younger's own draught IPA, with a fairly high original gravity of 1043, cost 13p or 13½p – far better value for money than the keg bitter. As for lager, both Tuborg and Carlsberg had gravities of 1030, yet they cost 22p and 18p respectively, an incredible state of affairs. As the *Sunday Mirror* said, 'we think these two lagers more suitable for a maiden aunt of moderate habits than for a man who uses his muscles.'

Prices change, and in the five years after 1972 they more or less doubled, but the relatively poor value of keg bitter (and especially of lager) compared with real draught beer remains the same. But a comprehensive survey by CAMRA went one step further by comparing prices (correct at 1 February 1977) for a large number of real draught beers of varying gravities – and it came up with a number of surprising anomalies. Ind Coope's Draught Burton Ale, for example, was 5½p more expensive than Gale's HSB – yet the Gale's beer is four degrees stronger. For ordinary bitter, 'Banks's, Boddington's, Hook Norton, Brain's and Welsh come out cheapest ... Bass Charrington, Allied Breweries and Whitbread come out worst.' In other words, the Big Six, supposedly the most efficient brewing companies, are normally charging consistently more for products which are weaker than some of those produced by their competitors. Viewed from another angle, the healthy competition of three local brewers in Nottingham (Hardy's & Hanson's, Home Brewery and Shipstone's) is reflected in very low prices: their milds, all relatively strong and almost always served traditionally, are virtually the cheapest in the country. The evidence is sometimes complex, but one inescapable fact emerges time after time – in addition to being unrivalled in terms of flavour and quality, a pint of real draught beer is also quite clearly the best value for money.

2 A History of Brewing in Britain

Beer, as has already been noted, had become a part of everyday life in Mesopotamia by about 3000 B.C., and there is archaeological evidence that barley had by then been cultivated for two thousand years. It seems likely that the process of malting originally developed as a way of improving the food value and the taste of grain, and that the making of 'beer-bread' (cakes of malted barley) was the first step in the history of brewing. Malted barley, though, must be fermented to produce beer; it is probable that the first fermented drinks resulted from the spontaneous fermentation of honey or natural fruit juices, and either that observation of this phenomenon led to experiments in the fermentation of malt, or that fermentation occurred accidentally through the re-use of a vessel whose cracks had become infected with yeast. What is certain is that the resulting beer bore little resemblance to its modern equivalent, not least because honey and spices appear to have been added to it, and it would therefore be thick, sweet and cloying.

The separate arts of cereal cultivation, malting and fermentation spread slowly westwards from the Middle East, and it is likely that barley was cultivated in England by 3000 B.C. There is no proof, however, that it was used in making beer at this time, although there is documentary evidence that the practice of brewing was firmly established by the time of the Roman invasion. Beer (more correctly, unhopped ale) was unquestionably of prime significance as a source of nourishment – 'of vital importance to all men and women and probably children', according to Monckton in *A History of the English Public House* – during the Roman occupation and in succeeding centuries. Indeed, so great had the number of alehouses become by the tenth century that a decree had to be issued limiting them to one per village.

Early medieval brewing took place in wooden vessels, with the single exception of the open copper, heated from fires lit directly beneath it, and made of copper. The Queen's College Brewery in Oxford, modelled around a fourteenth-century brewhouse, included an oak mash tun, an underback where the wort was collected after it had been separated from the spent grains, a sixteenth-century hand pump which was used to raise the wort into the copper, wooden cooling troughs and fermenters, and oak casks in which the fermentation was completed. The 'ordinary' ale produced at Queen's College had an original gravity of 1070, and the Chancellor's Ale, brewed to mark special occasions, was virtually double that strength!

From the end of the twelfth century onwards local and national taxes were levied on ale and these were increasingly accompanied by legislation aimed at safeguarding the drinker: the Assize of Ale in 1266, which established fixed prices for ale, and the appointment of ale conners to judge the strength and quality of ale are two examples. By the end of the fourteenth century, ale was sold in three types of premises: inns which offered food and accommodation as well as ale, taverns (which also sold wine), and alehouses. Nevertheless, it appears that only about one-tenth of total ale production at this time was accounted for in this way, the vast majority of ale, especially in country areas, being brewed and consumed in the home.

Water, yeast and malt were the only permitted constituents of commercially-brewed ale and there were heavy penalties for those caught adulterating their ale. Given this background, it is hardly surprising that the introduction of hops in the fifteenth century met with fierce opposition (indeed, their introduction was resisted in every country in Europe, partly on commercial grounds). The cultivation of hops is first recorded in the Hallertau area in 736, but their spread was evidently rapid, since they were grown in the Ile-de-France in 822 and around Prague by the eleventh century.

Yet there is no evidence of hops in England until 1400, in which year hopped beer from Holland was imported through the port of Winchelsea, although there is clear evidence that Dutch brewers were well established in the south-east soon afterwards. Beer brewers are mentioned as distinct from ale brewers in Hythe in 1419, and they were brewing in Southwark by 1440. There was a good deal of resistance to the spread of hopped beer, with the formation of the Brewers' Company in 1437 to represent the interests of ale brewers, and as late as 1519 brewers in Shrewsbury were prohibited from adding hops to the brew. But by the early sixteenth century beer brewers were strongly established in both Canterbury and London, largely at the expense of those brewing unhopped ale, and the acceptance of hopped beer gradually spread through the country. There were, of course, notable advantages to the brewer and publican in dealing with beer rather than ale: because of the preservative properties of the hops, beer could be kept in good condition for a longer period than ale, and since it could be brewed at a lower gravity (ale had to be brewed strong to make it keep at all) it could be produced from fewer raw materials, giving a higher profit margin. Beer was probably only about half the strength of ale in the sixteenth century, requiring about two bushels of malt per barrel compared with about four or five bushels for ale.

The use of hops in brewing prepared the way for a second fundamental change in the industry. Common brewers – those who sold their beer in bulk to publicans rather than selling it all retail – were in existence by the middle of the fourteenth century, but while their main trade was in unhopped ale they were unable to expand much, since their product had to be sold quickly before it deteriorated, and so could not be transported over long distances. Hopped beer, however, was a much more stable product which enabled the more adventurous commercial breweries to increase production and expand their market area. By 1578 there were twenty-six common brewers in London and Westminster, with a particularly high concentration in Southwark, and three of these between them used 2,000 loads of wood a year to heat their open coppers. At this time most production was still in the hands of publican-brewers, but little more than a hundred years later there were 194 common brewers in London and their combined production totalled 962,000 barrels of strong beer and ale, and 690,000 barrels of small beer, compared with only about 6,000 barrels of each produced by the publican-brewers.

The introduction of excise duty on beer was heralded by the imposition of a levy of fourpence a quarter on malt by James I in 1614. The Civil War, which began in 1642, provided the necessary impetus and in the following year the Parliamentarians imposed a duty of two shillings per barrel on beer retailing at six shillings a barrel or more, and a duty of sixpence per barrel on cheaper beer. In 1645 Charles I followed this example. After the Restoration there were moves to abolish the duty, and the Brewers' Company petitioned Parliament for the removal of 'the illegal and intolerable burden of Excise', but without success. In fact the government took quite the opposite course of action, recognizing that beer duty was a convenient method of raising revenue, and by 1689 duty on strong beer was 3s. 3d. Ten years later the duty on strong beer had reached five shillings per barrel, a level at which it remained for the next fifty years.

Two central developments characterized the brewing industry in the eighteenth century: first, the introduction of a completely new product, porter, and second (though closely linked to the rise of porter) the emergence of large firms which came to dominate brewing in a way which had been totally absent hitherto. Before the emergence of porter, the range of beer available in London alehouses included stout butt beer (the strongest beer on the market), strong brown ale, common brown ale, pale and amber beers, and small beer; the words 'ale' and 'beer' were now both used to describe hopped liquor, and the production of unhopped ale had virtually ceased. Beers from two or more casks were often mixed, and one such mixture, consisting of new and stale brown ales and pale ale, was known as 'three threads'. It was a tedious business for the publican to draw beer from three casks to satisfy a single customer, and Ralph Harwood, a partner in the Bell Brewhouse at Shoreditch, is credited with the idea of brewing one beer which combined the merits of all three. The new beer, originally called 'entire' in that it was drawn entirely from one cask, was first brewed in the autumn of 1722. It was brewed from brown malts, and was therefore dark and thick, and it was also relatively heavily hopped, so that it was more bitter to the palate than the brown ales with which it had to compete.

The new beer was immediately successful and became especially popular with London porters and labourers – hence the name of porter. By 1726 it had clearly won a considerable proportion of the London market – indeed, a visitor to the capital noted that 'there are a number of houses where nothing but this sort of beer is sold.' There were a number of reasons for the success of porter, quite apart from its intrinsic merit. In particular, the retail price of porter, which was originally threepence per quart, undercut both 'twopenny' ale at fourpence per quart and the high-quality pale ales which had been introduced fairly recently and were gaining in popularity. Yet the extra costs involved in porter brewing were considerable, because the new beer had to be matured in casks or vats for much longer than conventional beers, and this required greater stocks, a greater amount of cellarage, more casks and more labour. The explanation of this apparent paradox is that porter was the first beer which was ideal for mass production, so that the larger common brewers could derive economies of scale as their production increased – a point which will be returned to later.

At first porter was matured for up to a year or more before it was sent out, although it became possible to reduce this period after the process of fining beer with isinglass to help to clarify it was introduced (though, since porter was a dark beer, this was of less importance than for fine pale ales). Initially, too, porter was of greater apparent strength than the brown ales, although the strength of porter was progressively reduced in the later eighteenth century in an attempt to keep the price stable despite increasing duty and raw material costs. It was never particularly important to use the finest malt or hops for porter, since imperfections were less easily noticed than in pale ales. Porter brewing spread throughout the country, and is mentioned in Sheffield in 1744 and as far away as Glasgow in 1795. The Bristol Porter Brewery was founded by Philip George by 1788. Its popularity was unquestioned; in 1758 it was said that 'Beer, commonly called porter, is become almost the universal cordial of the populace.'

Yet within a century of its introduction porter was suffering from declining demand, and became extinct in Britain. Although some of the leading ale brewers in London were beginning to brew porter in the 1830s, it is more significant that porter brewers were turning to ale at the same time. Whitbread's, for example, one of the leading porter brewers, began to brew other beers in 1834. By this time there was a pronounced switch in public demand in favour of the paler beers, notably those produced in Burton-on-Trent, and it is no coincidence that the leading porter brewers of London, where the brewing water was less suitable for brewing pale ales, were setting up their own breweries in Burton in the middle of the nineteenth century: Ind Coope in 1856, Charrington's in 1871 and Mann & Crossman in 1875. The market for porter contracted steadily from the 1830s onwards, although it was still produced by most breweries at the start of the twentieth century.

Despite its relatively short life, porter made possible the rise of the major brewers. Though most of the beer produced in London in 1700 was brewed by common brewers, no single firm had grown to any significant extent, so that few were brewing more than 5,000 barrels a year. A century later six London porter brewers were producing over 100,000 barrels a year, and Barclay Perkins, Whitbread and Meux Reid were brewing about twice this amount. The two Calvert brothers, who ran independent breweries which were later united, were the first to reach an annual output of 50,000 barrels, in 1748; Whitbread reached the 200,000 barrel mark in 1796; and Barclay Perkins led the way to 300,000 barrels in 1815. The sheer size of these enterprises, in terms of plant, raw materials and labour was phenomenal, and the speed of their growth was not to be equalled until 'merger mania' set in during the 1960s. Such growth was not universally acceptable; Professor Bradley, writing in 1727, remarked on the high proportion of publican-brewers in northern counties, and claimed that 'in all these counties it is as rare to find ill malt liquors as it is to find good in London.'

By 1748 considerable concentration had occurred in the London brewing industry, to the extent that almost half the beer produced was brewed in twelve brewhouses. It is almost certain that this process of concentration had hardly started in the provinces, largely because the smaller markets involved provided less incentive to the new breed of brewing entrepreneurs. The growth of some of the twelve market leaders in London illustrates the trend of the industry, and incidentally highlights the decline of the smaller brewers, hemmed in by legislation and taxation on one side, and on the other, unable to compete with larger firms who could brew more efficiently and command more capital to expand the business. The birth of Whitbread's brewery, for example, was unremarkable, though its early growth was exceptional. Samuel Whitbread was sent to London in 1736 to be apprenticed to a leading brewer, John Wightman, at a fee of £300. Six years later Whitbread established a business in a relatively small brewery on Old Street, in partnership with Thomas and Godfrey Shewell. Production at this time was around 18,000 barrels per annum, and thirteen public houses, together with the brewery taps adjacent to the two brewhouses, were purchased as a basis for the business.

Within eight years Whitbread had achieved such success that a site in Chiswell Street was bought and developed as a porter brewery, with the Old Street and adjacent Goat brewhouses retained to produce pale and amber beers. The famous porter tun room at the Chiswell Street brewery, whose roof span was exceeded only by Westminster Hall, had been constructed by 1760. The number of public houses on the rent roll had increased from the original thirteen to twenty-four by 1756, and to eighty by the end of the eighteenth century. Well before this Whitbread's output had reached 120,000 barrels a year of porter alone, and the position of the firm as the leading brewers in the country was reflected in a royal visit to the brewery in 1787. Profits fluctuated with the cost of raw materials, but after an initial period of utter devotion to the business, ploughing back all spare funds into the drive for expansion, Whitbread was able to move into the property market in Bedfordshire in 1761, and by 1799 £350,000 had been diverted from the business for the purpose of building up a country estate.

Of rather greater antiquity was the Anchor Brewhouse in Southwark, which was in operation by 1616, and which passed into the hands of James Child, from whom Edmund Halsey – initially a labourer, later a clerk and eventually, after his marriage to Child's daughter, salaried manager – inherited the business in 1696. Under Halsey the brewery became one of the most important in London, and at his death it was bought by his clerk and nephew, Ralph Thrale, for £30,000, a sum which he paid off in a mere eleven years from the profits. In 1750, the production of 46,000 barrels equalled that of Truman's, the most consistently successful of the porter brewers at that time, but eight years later the barrelage was only 33,000 – a reflection on the fact that too much had been taken out of the business to sustain the standard of living of Thrale and his son. Both Whitbread and Truman's produced 60,000 barrels annually by now, and the moral is clear: without a driving force utterly devoted to the business, inefficient methods and neglect lead to declining trade and production.

Many of the surviving names in the brewing industry date from the second half of the eighteenth century (together, of course, with a vast number which have been more or less completely submerged in later amalgamations). In London, apart from those already mentioned, Charrington and Moss established themselves at the Anchor Brewery, Mile End, in 1766; Courage at Horselydown, Southwark, in 1789; and the Stag Brewery in Pimlico, established in 1636, eventually passed to Watney in 1836, having been rescued from financial disaster by Elliott in 1787. Elsewhere, Worthington began brewing in Burton in 1744, and Guinness in Dublin in 1759. Between 1750 and 1800 the number of brewers increased from 996 to 1,382, a graphic illustration of the opportunities available for common brewers to establish themselves in a market which was ripe for expansion. By 1800, though, the larger brewers had already progressed to such a size that new firms were likely to be deterred from entering the industry, since in their early years they could not hope to gain the same economies of scale. The story of the Golden Lane Brewery, examined in detail by Peter Mathias in *The Brewing Industry in England 1700–1830*, illustrates the problems of new enterprises.

The 'Genuine Beer Brewery' in Golden Lane was launched in the premises formerly containing Michael Combrune's brewery in 1805, at a time when the leading brewers were under fire for raising the price of porter; one of their number retorted that they held no monopoly, but were successful because of the quality of their product. Then, as now, this was hardly fair: the only way to compete was to attain the same size as the established giants of the industry, and yet these giants had by now begun to acquire tied houses, and in any case were in control of the free trade. The sponsors of the Golden Lane brewery decided, however, to attempt to match the capital employed by the leading brewers, and attracted sufficient backing (partly from publicans) to commence brewing. The first beer, described as 'a genuine article from malt and hops only', was sent out in October 1805 and was sold at a price lower than that charged by the leading brewers. The initial success was astonishing, production in the first three years totalling 57,400 barrels, 125,700 barrels and 131,600 barrels respectively. In the third year only Barclay Perkins and Meux Reid produced more. The effect on the leading porter brewers was considerable, in terms of price competition and quality of product, and it is not inconceivable that some of their number were involved in the legal action which indirectly led to the downfall of the Golden Lane brewery.

The brewery did, in fact, survive its legal battles, first over the legality of publicans acting as partners in the firm, and second over an extraordinary prosecution for supposedly adulterating beer with isinglass finings. The commercial basis of the firm, however, became markedly less secure with increases in the price of raw materials between 1807 and 1813 – increases which were particularly severe on a low-price brewery which received less from publicans for its beer than did other breweries. The payment of high dividends provided a further strain, and the implications are that cash problems, costs of materials, and inability to secure a worthwhile tied trade caused a rapid decline. Production had fallen to 50,000 barrels a year by 1813, and it became necessary to weaken the beer to maintain the price differential. The efforts of rival brewers to exclude the Golden Lane brewery from the tied trade proved increasingly successful, and the firm never recovered, the premises being sold in 1826 and later demolished.

Perhaps the critical problem was the encroachment of the brewers on the retail trade, a development which had started in the early years of the eighteenth century, although at that time the acquisition of tied houses was unusual and there was no great enthusiasm for the practice on the part of the brewers, since it tied up part of their working capital without producing a tangible return. On the other hand, it is evident that as early as 1686 considerable numbers of publicans were in debt to the brewers who supplied them, and it is easy to envisage loans or mortgages being arranged, with the publican's property as security for the transaction; should the publican's business fail, the brewer had little option but to take over the alehouse.

Nevertheless, until about 1800 there was no real incentive for the common brewers actively to pursue a policy of buying up outlets for their beer, since new alehouses could easily be opened and most publicans were in any case in the habit of buying their beer year after year from the same supplier – purely from the point of view of mutual convenience.

Despite this relative stability, smaller brewers were still being forced out of the industry, and publican-brewers were ceasing to produce their own ale, for economic reasons, since neither could compete with the giant common brewers who derived significant economies of scale from their vast production of porter. The process was intensified when the scramble for tied houses began in earnest around 1800, for two main reasons: much more restrictive licensing policies on the part of the Justices of the Peace, from about 1790 onwards, together with the economic factors such as bad harvests, war taxation and a decline in demand. The result was an unprecedented interest in gaining a tied estate, coupled with the knowledge that tied houses would now have a virtual local monopoly, since new licences nearby would not be allowed in a period of restrictive licensing. Less efficient and less aggressive brewers were soon eliminated; one-third of the 150 breweries operating in London in 1790 had ceased brewing by 1815. By the following year 14,200 out of 48,000 alehouses in England and Wales belonged to the brewers, and half of London's alehouses had become tied. Already there were complaints about the spread of tied trade, and the House of Commons Committee on Public Breweries, reporting in 1819, 'found no evidence that the consumer had been injured in any way but objected to the monopoly which the brewers were creating.'

The evidence suggests that in 1810 Thrale's supplied 477 public houses in London, of which 277 were tied; Whitbread 308, with 256 tied; and Truman's 481, of which 378 were tied. This is in one sense an impressive set of statistics, showing that brewers had recognized that their huge capital commitment on plant, equipment and stocks necessitated an equal commitment in terms of assured outlets for their products. The reverse side of the picture is less palatable, in that the various factors of taxation and competition were leading to the withdrawal from the industry of publican-brewers and of private brewing, which accounted for about half of beer production in 1800 but which had become extinct except in areas such as the Black Country a century later. Between 1800 and 1900 the number of publican-brewers declined by about three-quarters to less than 10,000, and in the early twentieth century their decline was even more dramatic, to only about 2,000 by the beginning of the First World War.

The rise of the major brewing companies was inexorable, and a number of new features became apparent in the middle of the nineteenth century. First, Burton-on-Trent, always an important centre, took on even greater prominence with the coming of the railways and the resultant expansion of brewers such as Worthington and Bass. Second, the London brewers recognized the coming popularity of pale ale, and constructed or bought breweries in Burton, a practice which was a step on the way to the notion of national brewing concerns. The increasing scale of the largest brewers led in the 1880s to the flotation of many of them as public companies, with even greater financial abilities as a consequence. The battle for outlets intensified, and the value of alehouses was doubled or even trebled as the major firms fought among themselves for a declining number of free outlets. In such a climate it was hardly surprising that recessions saw the demise of some companies, and saw others coming together for mutual protection – Mitchell's merger with Butler's in Birmingham in 1898 being one example. By 1914 the struggle for control of outlets was virtually over, and Monckton goes so far as to suggest that 95 per cent of public houses were tied by this date – surely an over-estimate, but indicative of the brewers' stranglehold on the retail side of the trade.

There were, of course, areas where independence and competition survived rather longer, especially where traditions of publican-brewers and domestic brewing were strongest. The decline of brewing by publicans was, for example, very slow in Leeds and the surrounding district, but the most striking exception to the rule of dominance by common brewers was Birmingham, where even in the 1880s common brewers accounted for only a quarter of production. In fact in 1873, 97 per cent of the public houses and beerhouses in Birmingham held a brewing licence. Brewing was often in the hands of outside brewers, visiting once or twice a week to brew in outhouses or even in the cellars, but nevertheless a distinctive product was on sale in most Birmingham pubs. The city therefore maintained its tradition of individuality, independence and the fostering of small enterprises even in its brewing industry. But the national trend could not be denied for ever, and when it began the decline of publican brewing was devastatingly rapid. By 1893 less than a fifth of Birmingham's pubs had a brewing licence, and thereafter the practice subsided unremarked. The overriding reason was the restriction on new licences, which led, as elsewhere, to a stampede from brewers anxious to ensure outlets for their beer. In 1890 the Holt Brewery Company held 155 pubs, and had already absorbed several smaller companies. Mitchell's, soon to merge with Butler's, had 88 pubs, and Ansell's were third on the list with 64. The publican-brewer could not compete; in 1888 it was said that 'there had been a tremendous run on free houses, and in the course of a short time there would scarcely be a house worth buying in the market.'

An impressive range of beer was available to nineteenth-century drinkers (the Stafford Brewery offered ten different beers in cask in 1855, for example), and they were relatively strong, too. Three types of Burton ale, with original gravities between 1077 and 1120, are listed in 1843, and the strengths of common ale (1073) and porter (1050) clearly show that the most popular beers were also potent. Its characteristics at this time were judged to be its complete lack of sweetness and high hopping rate; porter was now often coloured with patent black malt, and strong porter had become known as brown stout; drinkers were warned against the 'intoxicating and stupyfying (*sic*) qualities' of strong ales. A notable influence from 1847 was the addition of sugar, which was first permitted on a regular basis at this time. Previously the only permitted ingredients had been malt, hops, yeast and water (it is a matter of regret, as noted in Chapter 1, that Britain failed to imitate Bavaria's Reinheitsgebot or Purity Law of 1516, now mandatory throughout West Germany, which restricts the raw materials of German beer to hops, barley and water). The average original gravity of beer in 1880 was 1057, and it fell only very slowly to 1053 in 1905. The effect of the First World War was to reduce the average to about 1040, and savagely to increase the incidence of excise duty: not just for the duration of the war, either, since 'good strong beer at low prices was a casualty of the conflict.' Lower gravities were accompanied by a decrease in the hopping rate, and so the product became weaker and sweeter. The Second World War merely accelerated this decline.

The development of the larger common brewers in the eighteenth century, and the acceleration in the acquisition of tied houses in the nineteenth century, form the historical basis for the sickness gripping the present-day brewing industry. Neither trend could logically be opposed at the time, in the one case because of the economies of large-scale production and in the other because of the financial difficulties of publicans; brewers were by no means eager to take on tied houses until licensing restrictions made it imperative. But there comes a point at which the logic of concentration is denied by more powerful forces; where the public interest is challenged by such concentration, and where the giants of the industry are confronted by diseconomies of production and dissatisfaction over tied houses and all that they stand for. Such a point has been reached and passed in British brewing; the next chapter traces the route followed by the brewing giants and outlines the present malaise from the consumer's point of view.

3 Mergers and Mediocrity: The Growth of the Big Six

The closure of a town's brewery can have a catastrophic local effect, not only upon sources of employment in the area, but upon the character and atmosphere of local pubs, and on the choice and quality of beer available to local drinkers. All too often the decision to close down is taken not in the town affected, but in company boardrooms hundreds of miles away, isolated from local preferences and insulated from local ill-feeling. Joule's brewery in Stone, Staffordshire, is just one of hundreds of examples in the last two decades of victims of the policies of rationalization, centralization and pursuit of apparent efficiency by the big brewers – policies which are now seen to have been hopelessly misguided, yet which have dealt an irreparable blow to the beer drinker's heritage.

The town of Stone has been associated with brewing since the twelfth century, when monks started producing ale on the site later used by Joule's. Indeed, the firm of Joule's was itself in existence by the end of the eighteenth century, and quickly built up a considerable reputation for the quality of its beers. Joule's first mistake, perhaps, was to agree to a takeover by Bass Charrington in the late 1960s. At first the indications were that all was well (though the long-term future of the brewery was always uncertain). As late as 1968 Joule's chairman was able to claim that, although the company was a subsidiary of Bass Charrington, 'there had been no material changes in the day-to-day running of the brewery.' Less than two years later the brewery's impending closure was announced – a fairly material change, and one which must surely have been under consideration at the time of the chairman's statement quoted above. Early in 1974 the brewery was closed, despite last-minute appeals to common sense and a protest march in the town. Bass Charrington had given an assurance that Joule's bitter would be brewed at Burton-on-Trent, and would be identical to the traditional Stone brew, but few local drinkers would agree. Many feel that the taste is different and the beer is weaker: one brewery worker (one of a hundred whose jobs were lost in the closure) commented, 'It's just not the same now. In the old days you could sup eight or nine pints and it would not hurt you, but three pints of it nowadays plays hell with your stomach.'

The story of Joule's is symptomatic of the disease which affected the big brewers in the 1960s – a decade which saw the loss of 147 breweries (and there were only 358 operating in January 1960, so that 41 per cent went to the wall in ten years) and which saw the seven major brewers increase their market share from 45 per cent to 75 per cent. By 1970, then, they had forced their way into a position of domination in the industry, able through aggressive marketing policies to create their own demand for products which were convenient for them to produce, rather than genuinely demanded by drinkers. Similarly they were able to shut down local breweries and concentrate brewing in supposedly efficient large modern beer factories. Indeed, at the time Joule's brewery was closed, the big brewers were going ahead with plans to shut down another seventeen breweries around the country, with a total lack of concern for local feeling.

The decision to close down Barnsley Brewery was a prime example of this lack of sensitivity on the part of the giant brewers, whose ear was by this time so far from the ground that disquiet in the public bar passed completely unnoticed.

Barnsley bitter was renowned for its strength and flavour ('the brew that felled the strongest' was a particularly apt description) and almost revered in south Yorkshire. The brewery was taken over by John Smith's of Tadcaster in 1962, but there appeared to be no grounds for concern, especially when a 'major redevelopment' of the brewery was announced for 1966–7. When John Smith's closed its Newark brewery (formerly run by Warwick & Richardson in 1967 Barnsley bitter was introduced as a replacement in some East Midlands pubs and was 'well received in its new trading areas'. Yet five years or so later Courage – which had by now acquired John Smith's and, ironically, had themselves been swallowed by Imperial Tobacco – was claiming that the brewery was decrepit and inefficient, incapable of modernization, and therefore doomed to closure. Howls of protest from devotees of the brew, a march around the town organized (as at Stone) by the Campaign for Real Ale, and a denunciation of the closure by the local MP, Roy Mason, predictably had little effect in changing a decision which was probably irrevocable by the time customers were informed.

As has been said, this sort of arrogant decision, resulting in a loss of satisfaction and choice for local consumers, was repeated scores of times in the 1960s and early 1970s; in some ways it merely intensified the process which had begun with the sustained growth of the common brewers and their rapid acquisition of tied houses from the eighteenth century onwards. Nevertheless, this early transformation of the industry was less dramatic, and could be accommodated without causing the serious problems faced by drinkers nowadays. There were, in fact, still some 6,500 breweries operating in 1900, and since many of these were extremely small concerns – publicans brewing their own beer, for example – it was inevitable that, when the advantages of obtaining beer from the common brewers became more apparent, the number of breweries would fall considerably. Of the 3,000 breweries which were active at the end of the First World War, therefore, only 700 were still in existence by 1945. Yet, fifteen years later, there were still 358 breweries (owned by 247 separate firms), and a considerable degree of choice was still available in most areas of the country. Furthermore, although a number of beers were by now nationally known and widely available (Bass, for example, and Guinness), there were no brewers with a truly national distribution of tied houses, and most companies had tightly defined local or regional trading areas.

Between 1960 and 1971, however, the structure of the brewing industry was dramatically altered by a spate of mergers and takeovers which created a handful of national brewers with enormous concentrations of breweries, pubs and power. Astonishingly, around 150 companies ceased to trade independently during this period. Some chose to seek an 'association' with a larger brewer; others tried desperately but unsuccessfully to remain independent. The real incentive for the big brewers, given that demand was rising only very slowly, was the extra tied houses gained in such takeovers – giving more scope, through increased numbers of outlets and larger distribution areas, to other developments such as mass advertising of 'national' premium beers. The breweries gained in these takeovers were of less use and were normally closed, regardless of the loss of distinctive beers with strong local followings; after a period of local opposition, though, 'the customer accepts as a fait accompli that his favourite brew is no longer available' – he has little choice to do otherwise.

In 1960, then, the seven largest brewers produced 45 per cent of the beer brewed in the United Kingdom. By 1969 this share had risen to three-quarters, and by 1972 to four-fifths. Six of the seven had also built up (to a greater or lesser degree) nation-wide chains of pubs offering for the most part heavily promoted but bland and insipid products with premium price tags. The first steps had been taken in the late 1950s. Sir Charles Clore's bid in 1959 for Watney's, though it proved unsuccessful, provoked the major brewers – horrified by the thought of brewing companies controlled by outsiders rather than by members of the 'beerage', the closely knit group of families who had historically led the industry – into a spate of mergers in an effort to grow too big to be swallowed by outside bidders. (Ironically, even this tactic was to fail to save Watney's when it was next assailed by a bidder thirteen years later: Grand Metropolitan Hotels successfully added Watney's to their clutch of subsidiary interests.) In 1961 Ind Coope, Ansell's and Tetley's merged to form Allied Breweries, the first truly national brewing company, combining Ind Coope's interests in Scotland and south-east England with Tetley's empire on both sides of the Pennines and Ansell's territory in the Midlands and South Wales. Six years later the merger of Bass, Mitchell's & Butler's with Charrington United Breweries created Bass Charrington, the largest brewing company in Europe.

The rise and rise of Bass Charrington from modest beginnings in Burton-on-Trent in 1744 to its present exalted position provides a fascinating insight into the progressive concentration of the brewing industry. It was in 1744 that William Worthington established a brewery in the High Street in Burton – the fourth commercial brewing enterprise to be started in the town. Thirty-three years later, William Bass, previously a haulage contractor, moved into the brewing business with conspicuous success. Both Bass and Worthington sold their products mostly in the export market, although some was available locally, but in 1827 the celebrated auction of shipwrecked casks of Bass India Pale Ale in Liverpool led (so the story goes) to the fame of Bass and Worthington beers spreading throughout the country. Their distribution was aided enormously by the arrival of the Midland railway in Burton in 1840 – and, with the acquisitiveness and commercial instinct which was to be built upon by his successors, Michael Bass took a stake in the railway company, became one of its directors, and even saw to it that the cellars at St Pancras station were laid out to accommodate hogsheads of draught Bass.

Output increased rapidly during the nineteenth century, from 2,000 barrels a year in 1797 to almost a million barrels per annum in 1877, and necessitated an almost continuous programme of building and re-building. The Bass New Brewery, opened in 1863, remains the largest single brewery producing real draught beer in the country. In 1926 Bass and Worthington merged to form the dominant company in Burton. Thirty-five years later, after a further series of takeovers, Bass, Ratcliff & Gretton, as it was then known, combined with Mitchell's & Butler's and thereby established themselves as the largest brewing company in the Midlands, since M & B had pursued a policy of buying up most of the local competition in and around Birmingham – such as Highgate Brewery in Walsall, Butler's Springfield Brewery in Wolverhampton, and a host of others in Birmingham itself.

The Charrington family had entered the brewing industry in a rather different way, by taking over the Anchor Brewery in Mile End, London, in the latter part of the eighteenth century. In an area where porter brewing was dominant, Charrington's was the leading ale brewer, and it began to brew porter as well in 1833. To take advantage of the water at Burton, it decided to set up a brewery there in 1871, purely to supply pale ale to its tied houses, which were still concentrated in and around London. Indeed, despite a large number of twentieth-century acquisitions, Charrington's remained firmly London-based until 1962, when it was persuaded to merge with Northern United Breweries, the conglomeration of sixteen breweries acquired in the two previous years by the Canadian entrepreneur, Eddie Taylor.

The geographical extent of Taylor's buying spree was certainly impressive: the list for 1960 included – amongst others – Sheffield (Hope & Anchor Breweries), Tadcaster (Hammond's), Falkirk (Aitken's), South Wales (Webb's of Aberbeeg), and, in 1961, breweries in Blackpool, Manchester, Grimsby and Northern Ireland. The new company, Charrington United Breweries, was not so much a national company as a collection of small breweries with no overall cohesion or logic. The opportunities for rationalization were enormous, and it was not long before they were seized.

By 1964, decisions had clearly been taken on how to reorganize the company's brewing capacity, and some modernization had been carried out: 'these improvements have enabled the company to shut down some of the smaller and older breweries,' in the words of the annual report. During 1964 breweries at Alloa, Brighton, Hull, London (Woodhead's South London Brewery) and Yeovil were closed during what was described as 'a year of consolidation' and, by the following May, bids had already been made for Dunmow Brewery and Offiler's of Derby. Merger mania had set in by now, of course, and in 1967 John Charrington, still at that time the chairman, declared that the company would 'aim for further takeovers to speed progress.'

Bass, Mitchell's & Butler's were almost equally prominent in the merger race, absorbing Hunt Edmunds of Banbury in 1965 (and shutting down the quite substantial brewery there two years later), although they were at pains to demonstrate the selective nature of their acquisitions, since it was their view in 1965 that 'some small-sized firms are overvalued', with run-down properties and impoverished beer. A few months later John Young, chairman of Young's of Wandsworth, returned the fire: 'An impression given recently that some small-sized brewery concerns are overvalued and that in some instances properties have been neglected, and the quality of beers impoverished, is completely refuted.' But their reservations about the wisdom of take-overs failed in 1967 to stop Bass from putting in a rival, and ultimately successful, bid for Bent's of Liverpool, who were already under siege from Watney Mann's £17 million offer.

Later in 1967, however, Bass themselves were the target for Eddie Taylor, whose aspirations (stemming originally from his desire to gain outlets for his Canadian lager, Carling Black Label) were seemingly limitless. And on 21 July, Bass Charrington was formed as a result of 'the brewing merger of the century', a merger which escaped the attentions of the Monopolies Commission despite the fact that 11,000 pubs and one-fifth of the beer brewed in the country were now controlled by one company. Within a year of the Bass Charrington merger a further five breweries had been closed, and three more takeovers involving over a thousand pubs had been arranged – Stone's of Sheffield, Hancock's of Cardiff, and Joule's, whose sad capitulation has already been recorded.

In all, according to calculations produced by Keith Osborne of the Labologists' Society, some 273 breweries have been merged into one giant company, and since 1945 alone eighty-one takeovers have been involved. All but eleven of those 273 breweries have been closed, and nor can all of the surviving eleven be said to have an assured future, as we shall see. The beer drinker has been deprived, over a relatively short period of time, of hundreds of traditional beers – for example, not one of the beers previously produced at the sixteen breweries bought by Northern United in 1960–61 has survived. The replacement for all these local beers in the north had been Brew Ten, a weak, bland, and, by popular consensus, totally mediocre beer which even Bass Charrington officials now admit 'has never really gone well.' And yet in 1970 Brew Ten was 'launched to cater for the special local demand'!

Five of the northern breweries whose locally brewed beers made way for Brew Ten were in Lancashire: at Barrow, Blackpool, Burnley, Liverpool and Manchester. The reason for their closure was simple. Bass Charrington had decided to build an enormous beer factory in Runcorn, primarily because they were convinced that it would be more economical to brew in one place and transport beer all over the region than to brew in five places. Their plans were dogged by ill-fortune: a massive fire delayed the opening by several months, strikes by brewery workers disrupted production (a strike at one of the five redundant breweries might not have paralysed the other four, of course), the revival of demand for real draught beer meant that it had to be shipped in from Tadcaster, Sheffield and Burton (the projected demise of real ale had led to the decision that all beer brewed at Runcorn would be bright or keg), and, worst of all, between the planning of the Runcorn factory and its opening, the cost of transport rose sharply as the oil-exporting countries increased its price dramatically. Runcorn now stands as a monument to rationalization, capable of brewing two million pints a day – but none of it real draught beer; capable of supplying a very large area of the country – but at a crippling cost in petrol; and uniquely vulnerable to the disastrous effects of industrial action. As Chris Holmes, a former chairman of CAMRA, has said, 'I could guarantee that if Bass Charrington could change the decision they made several years ago they would never have built their factory at Runcorn. As other people have pointed out, it costs a lot to transport water around the country.'

A further irony of the Bass Charrington rationalization programme was the closure of the original Charrington plant in Mile End in 1975. The decision may well have hastened the departure, in February 1976, of the last Charrington on the board: this was, by now, anything but a family firm. The Mile End closure meant that Bass now had no brewery further south than Birmingham which could cater for their very large tied estate in the south-east. Beer for these pubs had to be ferried down from M & B in Birmingham (where most 'Charrington' Crown and IPA is brewed), Bass Worthington in Burton, or the new factory in Runcorn. Charrington beers have also been brewed at the Tolly Cobbold brewery in Ipswich, which at least reduces transport costs. The aim of the system, according to the Bass marketing organization, is flexibility: 'we have the ability to shift beer around the country as and when it is needed.' One wonders how that statement can be reconciled with claims that beers are brewed to cater for special local demand.

Historically, then, the activities of Bass Charrington during its transformation into a major brewing combine have hardly been calculated to appeal to the discerning consumer: small breweries have been ruthlessly eliminated, many locally popular beers have been discontinued and replaced by undistinguished regional or national brews, smaller or more remote pubs have often been closed (the company's annual meeting in 1970 was told that the 'policy of eliminating unprofitable premises continues') with little regard for the consequent hardships for drinkers and often for whole communities, and areas where Bass has monopoly power because of its control of a high proportion of pubs have suffered from restricted choice and, it appears, higher prices (compare the average price in Birmingham, where M & B owns about three out of every five pubs, with the adjacent Black Country, where there are still four independent brewers).

It is in the Black Country, incidentally, that Bass have kept open two small breweries which they must surely have been expected to rationalize out of existence years ago. The cynic might argue that Butler's brewery in Wolverhampton, which produces Springfield bitter, and the remarkable Highgate Brewery in Walsall, almost a cottage-industry concern, which brews the excellent Highgate mild in Britain's sole surviving mild-only brewery, survive only because of the fierce competition M & B face from the local breweries in the area. The Cape Hill brewery, which already supplies some beers to Springfield and Highgate pubs, surely has the capacity to supply all their beers, and the long-term future of the two breweries must be in doubt.

About a quarter of Bass Charrington's current production consists of real draught beer, and because of the immense scale of the company this represents more cask-conditioned beer than any other brewer in Britain. Few of the twenty different draught beers are widely respected, however, with honourable exceptions such as draught Bass, and if it is true that some of them are threatened, as suggested above, there may be a little cheer for the real beer drinker in Bass Charrington's future plans. There is further cause for concern, too, in the stakes which Bass hold in three of the smaller breweries. It has some 30 per cent of the share capital of Maclay's of Alloa, around 10 per cent of Higson's of Liverpool, and about one-third of Castletown Brewery on the Isle of Man. Minority stakes of this sort have in the past been converted into takeover bids; just as dangerous, however, is the possibility that a good offer from an outside bidder might be accepted for the financial gain involved. Bass had sizeable shareholdings in Cameron's and Tolly Cobbold (both bought by Ellerman Lines) and in Hull Brewery, acquired by Northern Foods, and each time accepted the offer for its shares.

A considerably different, but potentially more damaging and certainly more insidious, route to national prominence was followed by Whitbread. The early development of the firm was traced in some detail in Chapter 2; from the foundation of the firm in 1742 Whitbread rapidly became one of the leading London brewers, supplying 308 pubs by 1810. Although the firm continued to expand it remained based almost entirely in London, and as recently as 1960 owned only 2,000 pubs. Ten years earlier, however, Whitbread had begun their policy of association with local and regional brewers – the so-called 'umbrella' policy – and through their minority shareholdings in seventeen such firms they had an interest in a further 10,000 pubs by 1961. So wide had the net been cast that the Whitbread Investment Company was set up in 1956 purely to manage these holdings. In many cases independent firms had opted for the protection of Whitbread's umbrella as an insurance against takeover bids from the other major firms. The 1960s were to expose the folly of this approach.

In 1964 Colonel Whitbread was able to announce that the firm had trebled in size in the space of five years, though to disguise the predatory implications of this statement he was at pains to project an image of benevolence: 'some of the smaller breweries, especially those depending on family resources, have not had the financial strength' to continue in business, he explained. In 1963, for instance, Nimmo's of Castle Eden had joined the Whitbread group because it was 'a family-owned business which came to the conclusion that ... it would have to join up with a larger company'. During the preceding two years Tennant's of Sheffield, Flower's of Stratford and Luton, the City Brewery at Exeter, and West Country Breweries, a large regional combine based at Cheltenham, had all been absorbed. It is difficult to believe that all of them had been in desperate financial straits. The Colonel, still effusing benevolence, expanded on his policy of utilizing 'efficient, reasonably-sized breweries' in different parts of the country rather than one large brewery, and was able to make the claim – in hindsight, quite extraordinary – that 'the result of this has been that in the event of a merger we have seldom closed a brewery.'

Between 1960 and 1971 Whitbread closed no less than fifteen breweries, twenty-four bottling plants and fifty-four distribution depots, and became completely committed to a policy of producing keg beer and lager in a limited number of brand new beer factories located near motorways. Real draught beer is nowadays produced in a handful of the remaining traditional breweries, but Whitbread are obviously convinced that production and profits should be concentrated into their 'mega-keggeries', three of which (Luton, Samlesbury in Lancashire, and Magor in South Wales) have already been built, with a fourth apparently under consideration. Back in the mid-1960s, though, all this was speculation. The Whitbread umbrella was still, it appeared, an instrument of protection whereby family brewers could gain financial stability yet retain their independence. So when the directors of Archibald Campbell, Hope & King, of Edinburgh, invited Whitbread to enter into a trading agreement and make a financial investment in September 1965, the invitation was accepted with alacrity. Eighteen months later developments had taken a turn for the worse: activities had 'placed severe pressure on the already decreased profits'. Later in 1967 the inevitable takeover bid was accepted.

The image of benevolence was occasionally tarnished a little. After the death of their chairman, the directors of Cobb & Co., an old-established Margate brewery with about forty pubs in the Thanet area, stated their case: 'The directors wish it to be known that the company will continue as a private family business. They are confident that past achievements can not only be maintained but also show a substantial improvement in the future under personal control.' For whatever reasons, their confidence was misplaced; two years later Cobb's were part of the Whitbread group, which now controlled 8,550 pubs. In another two years the brewery was not only closed, depriving the Thanet populace of some excellent local beers, but also demolished, to the chagrin of Ian Nairn, writing in the *Sunday Times*: 'one of the best Georgian breweries in England ... all gone; the beer absorbed into the Whitbread umbrella – which here seems more like a vacuum cleaner – the brewery demolished in 1970. No developer seems interested in the resulting hole.'

Events in 1967 and 1968 further intensified this frenetic activity with both takeovers and closures. Rhymney Breweries and James Thompson (Barrow-in-Furness) had been absorbed in 1966. In May 1967 Threlfall's Chester's, with 826 pubs and breweries at Birkenhead, Liverpool and Salford, was bought for £24 million. Then came Campbell, Hope & King, closely followed by the Neath brewery of Evan, Evans Bevan, to bolster the South Wales tied estate (certainly the brewery was superfluous, and hence it was quickly shut down). Fremlin's, the major Kentish brewery, was bought in September, with a bid for Isaac Tucker of Gateshead accepted the following month. During the year 22 pubs had been opened and 116 closed, the deficit partly due to compulsory purchase orders, but also because pubs were now measured primarily in terms of profitability. The last brew at Mackeson's Hythe brewery (acquired years previously by Whitbread) took place in May 1968; with unconscious irony Whitbread announced that the last brew ceremony had taken placc in the room where the first beer had been produced in 1669. The ceremony was a prelude to a crowded summer. In June, Lacon's brewery at Great Yarmouth, bought three years previously, was closed. The following month saw Tomson & Wotton of Ramsgate, with 102 pubs, brought into the fold, bemoaning the modern economic pressures which had forced them to go to Whitbread (who already owned a third of the shares). Brewing was transferred to the former Fremlin's brewery in Maidstone within months. In August Bentley's Yorkshire Breweries, under the umbrella for ten years, were roped in, and the news broke that Flower's brewery in Stratford (despite considerable modernization) was to be closed early in 1969, with a loss of 450 jobs. In September Whitaker's of Halifax, another long-time associate, was taken over, adding another 135 pubs (the brewery was closed within months). Three months later John Young's was acquired to strengthen the Scottish operation. And the beginning of 1969 saw Strong's of Romsey taken over, together with its own subsidiaries, Wethered's of Marlow and Mew Langton on the Isle of Wight; a total of 940 pubs were bought in this one deal.

The vacuum cleaner's job was by now virtually complete: Whitbread's thirst for new outlets and new trading areas was apparently slaked, and when the Colonel retired in the summer of 1971 (a couple of months after Brickwood's of Portsmouth had been acquired in one last nostalgic deal) he was able to look back on a record of twenty-three mergers in eleven years, during which Whitbread's tied estate had grown from not much more than a thousand pubs to very nearly ten thousand. In the same time, of course, fifteen breweries had been closed and thousands of pubs had ceased to offer local drinkers the brews they were used to and which they wanted to drink. The spate of closures slowed to a trickle – Neath in May 1972, Maidstone in September 1972, for example – as the company consolidated its position and turned to the other main weapon in its creation of a new order, namely the development of major new beer factories. At the time the first of these, beside the M1 at Luton, reached full production in 1969, it was being suggested that 'the company's existing twenty-one breweries could be reduced to about seven in the next ten years.' Certainly the Luton plant led to the closure of the historic Chiswell Street brewery in 1975.

It was equally certain at the time that the mega-brewery at Samlesbury in the Lancashire green belt came on stream that it would replace the group's existing breweries in Blackburn, Salford and Liverpool. Such has been the demand for lager, however, that Samlesbury has been completely preoccupied with brewing so-called lager, and the three traditional breweries were reprieved, although sadly there was nothing traditional about the bright beer which is all that they turned out for four years after 1974. At that time Whitbread said that it was ready to respond to real demand for real draught beer, yet it stopped brewing it in the north-west; it has since had to install draught Bass in at least one of its Manchester tied houses to satisfy that demand, and in 1978 it began to brew real beer again at Liverpool and Salford – though at the same time it closed the Blackburn brewery. Construction of the third beer factory, at Magor, started in 1976 at an estimated cost of £30 million. As with Samlesbury, production was initially geared towards lager only, although the capacity to produce bright beer was also there.

By now Whitbread had three brand-new factories producing bright beer and lager (mainly the latter) and a motley collection of older breweries dotted around the country: three in the north-west, all producing bright beer only, and all threatened by the eventual expansion of Samlesbury; three in the north-east, with a handful of pubs supplied with draught beer from Castle Eden as the only sop to real beer drinkers; two in the south-east, at Marlow and Faversham; two in the south, at Romsey and Portsmouth – too close together to make too much long-term sense to the economies-of-scale men; two in the south-west, at Tiverton and Cheltenham; and one in Wales, at Cardiff. An intelligent crystal-ball gazer might forecast a fourth mega-brewery, and the likely area mentioned in the past has been around Basingstoke – hence posing a threat to some if not all of the four southern and south-eastern breweries; he might also predict further rationalization in the south-west and Wales (following the closure of Rhymney Brewery in 1978) when Magor expands, and also a tidying-up process in the north-east. Added to the likely demise of the older north-west breweries, that spells out a possible future of four or five very large breweries, producing no real draught beer at all, with perhaps a relic or two from the past (Wethered's, for instance) as a sop to traditionalists. Of course events may take a very different path: the economic circumstances of the past few years have slowed the investment in new plant, and may even have given the consumer revolution a chance to have influenced Whitbread. But the outlook is undoubtedly gloomy.

Still more worrying is the fact that the Whitbread umbrella, in the form of the Whitbread Investment Company, still has major shareholdings in a considerable proportion of Britain's surviving independent breweries, and smaller holdings in yet more. The list of major holdings at the start of 1978 was (as far as could be ascertained) as follows: Boddington's (26 per cent), Border (17), Brakspear (27), Buckley (18), Devenish (24), Marston's (33), Morland (39), Ruddle's (31). Minor holdings included Matthew Brown (5 per cent), Fuller's (3), Hardy's & Hanson's (6) and Wolverhampton & Dudley (7), with the probability of other undisclosed holdings. Whitbread therefore have a major say, usually through having one or more of their nominees on the board of directors, in the affairs of one in ten of Britain's remaining independent breweries. What we do not know, despite their potentially disastrous implications, are Whitbread's future intentions in respect of their holdings. In some cases, the stake held by Whitbread is so large that an eventual takeover seems very likely: Morland's, for example, are periodically the subject of bid rumours, and indeed the Whitbread shareholding has increased by a few per cent in recent years. Marston's, who already brew keg Tankard, might well be an attractive proposition if Whitbread needed more capacity for brewing beer, as opposed to lager. And it would be a tragedy if Boddington's, having fought off a takeover bid from Allied Breweries in 1970, were to fall to

Whitbread, who have doubled their stake in the last ten years.

The extraordinary thing about Whitbread is that despite its meteoric rise to national prominence, with often destructive side-effects, it retains a number of traditional breweries and a very fair selection of real draught beers – at least in the south of England. Fremlin's bitter from Faversham, the best bitter from the former Brickwood's brewery in Portsmouth (the beer is now renamed Pompey Royal), and the special bitter from Wethered's of Marlow are three examples of excellent traditional beers. But the company's view of them is confused, not least by their ludicrous policy – the weaknesses in which they now acknowledge – of labelling a dozen or so different beers, some keg and some draught, some weak and some strong, as Trophy bitter. Regrettably, Whitbread seems to be a company which, whilst ideally placed to offer a good choice of locally brewed real beer, is determined to ignore that opportunity and opt for bland beers produced in shining new factories, despite increasing evidence that this is exactly what the public doesn't want. The company refuses to be swayed, however, and emphasized this with the closure in 1978 of Rhymney Brewery, with the loss of two more cask-conditioned beers.

These two case histories of Bass Charrington and Whitbread serve to illustrate the dramatic and ruthless growth of the companies which have become known as the Big Six – the others being Allied Breweries, Courage, Scottish & Newcastle and Watney's (Guinness, though in the same league as a brewer, has only one tied house and is therefore a rather different concern). Individual methods of growth have varied; Scottish & Newcastle, for example, have shown a marked reluctance to step into the takeover market as a means of expansion, and in an unusually far-sighted forecast in 1967 their spokesman explained that this was because 'in our industry, the economies of size are, beyond a certain point, not particularly marked.' The free trade has therefore been the main target for S & N's energies, with a number of consequences. One has been to reduce the choice and quality of beer in many normally 'free' outlets, namely those which have negotiated loans with S & N and are therefore virtually tied to keg products such as Younger's Tartan – a sweet keg bitter which is low on gravity, low on hops, and low on just about everything else. Another has been the high concentration of outlets in Scotland and north-east England, which has meant that vast areas are without quality cask-conditioned beer, and which also, from the brewery's point of view, has depressed profits because of the low prices and high unemployment prevalent in the area. Allied, too, have rarely ventured into the takeover market, perhaps because of a wish to avoid a repetition of the humiliating rebuff they received from Boddington's – a victory for independence which is recounted in Chapter 4.

Watney's needs no introduction to the beer drinker; indeed, its extraordinary record in recent years has been explored so often that it need only be outlined here. Together with the ill-fated firm of Flower's, which was acquired and extinguished by Whitbread, as we have seen, Watney's was the pioneer of keg beer, and became so convinced that its Red Barrel was the shape of things to come that, in Richard Boston's memorable phrase, it put all its kegs in one basket and all but phased out traditional beer. Starting from a secure base built from numerous takeovers in and around London, Watney's reached outwards to envelop notable regional brewers in the 1960s. 1960 saw Phipps's of Northampton, Wilson's of Manchester and Usher's Wiltshire Brewery netted. Bullard's and Steward & Patteson were taken over in 1963, giving Watney's a stranglehold in Norwich (where they already owned the only other surviving brewery, Morgan's) which could not fail to work to the detriment of customers and, ultimately, to the embarrassment of Watney's themselves. Drybrough's added a Scottish side to the group in 1965; Beverley's of Wakefield was acquired in 1967.

Watney's policies at the beginning of the 1970s were clear: centralization and pressurization. Local identities were being submerged (hence Usher's best bitter was discontinued in 1969 so that the brewery could concentrate on the production of Watney's national brands) and the number of breweries in the group was being drastically pruned. Beverley's, for example, was closed in 1968, scarcely a year after being taken over; the official view was that 'rationalization of production was, and must remain, one of the main objects of amalgamation.' By a curious coincidence, the chairman of Hardy's & Hanson's, the independent Nottinghamshire brewery, was saying at virtually the same time, 'Every time a local brewery is taken over I think of it as one more fallen bastion, one step nearer to the charge of monopoly having some realistic meaning, one more step to total deadly monopoly through nationalization.'

By now, however, Watney's was involved in a headlong rush towards total rationalization, and it was unlikely to pay much attention to such remarks. Steward & Patteson's Ely brewery was closed in 1969, its Norwich brewery in 1970, and Bullard's Anchor brewery was axed in the same year. Development costing £2.2 million was completed at Watney's remaining Norwich brewery in 1971. In the same year another multi-million pound modernization was announced for Wilson's brewery in Manchester, as 'the next part of the group's long-term strategy aimed at reducing the brewing centres to four' – namely Norwich, Manchester, Edinburgh and Mortlake in west London. During the following year Watney's itself was taken over by Maxwell Joseph's Grand Metropolitan Hotels, after a protracted and often bitter battle, and the breweries of Truman's (already owned by

Grand Met) and Webster's of Halifax (cynically bought by Watney's in a desperate attempt to grow beyond the grasp of Grand Met), could be added to the list of those with a long-term future. Of the breweries to be retained, those at Edinburgh, Norwich, Mortlake and Brick Lane (Truman's) produced only keg and bright beers, a testimony to Watney's faith in its Red Revolution.

Watney's Red, the updated version of Red Barrel, was launched with an extraordinary fuss in the early 1970s. The advertising campaign which launched it was big, brash and above all enormously expensive, with well over £1 million spent on this single promotion. Pub signboards were painted red, interiors were refitted in red, new red dispense points costing over £100,000 were provided – and yet the new chilled, filtered, pasteurized, carbonated and pressure-dispensed beer failed to sell at all well. Watney's, with its keg-only policies in much of the country, its reliance on weak national beers, its attitudes to its tenants and its pubs, became the first major target for CAMRA. A market research survey carried out for the company gave the bad news; as their marketing director said, with heavy understatement, 'our image was not as desirable as we would have liked it to have been.' Profits were affected by the consumer revolution, so that 'a virulent word-of-mouth campaign' was blamed for the shortfall in performance.

So, incredibly, the policies went into reverse. The recipe for Usher's best bitter was disinterred, the beer went on sale again, and the future of the Trowbridge brewery, though not exactly assured, looked rather brighter than it had when its impending closure was announced in 1971. New beers were produced for the London market – Fined Bitter, a real draught beer with an original gravity of 1044, was brewed in Norwich and shipped to London (though none was sold locally, in the vast beer desert Watney's had created in Norfolk). Nine regional companies were set up, and although this led to some nonsenses, such as the creation of Mann's Northampton Brewery Company (a regional company with an old London brewer's name and with no brewery) it did serve to emphasize the new reliance on local beers such as those brewed by Wilson's, Webster's and Usher's. Anything, in fact, except Watney's: pubs that had been given the red facelift were quickly redecorated in any colour *except* red and attempts were made in some cases completely to disguise any association with Watney's. Allen Sheppard, chief executive, could admit in 1976 that 'now we know Big is Beautiful is no longer necessarily the best way to go about things – but at the time that just wasn't even visible.'

Relatively little adverse publicity has hit Courage, although its past record and present plans give cause for great concern over its lack of commitment to local breweries and to real draught beer. Its emergence as a national brewer was comparatively recent, and despite the acquisition of Simonds of Reading in 1960 and Bristol Brewery George's in 1961 the company remained heavily dependent on its trade in London and the south-east. The first indications that aspirations to national prominence were in mind came with the acquisition of James Hole of Newark in 1967. Much more significant was the merger with John Smith's Tadcaster brewery three years later, in a deal worth £33 million. Plymouth Breweries were bought in 1971 to extend the south-west trade, and in a series of pub swaps and deals Courage has tried to increase its strength in East Anglia, the West Midlands and North-West England, though it remains weak in some areas, and (like Scottish & Newcastle) is less significant than the other members of the Big Six. What is significant is the apparent policy of providing real draught beer only in the lucrative south and south-east (the Tadcaster and Newark plant provide bright beer only); and even this real beer is seriously threatened by the development of the brand-new Berkshire Brewery, destined to brew bright beer and lager only, which has doomed the Reading brewery and its superb best bitter and mild to extinction, and which might yet threaten the London, Bristol and Plymouth breweries if Courage opts for further expansion on a centralized basis.

The cumulative effect of the remarkable activity involving takeovers, mergers and subsequent brewery closures can be summarized in a number of telling statistics. We have already seen how 147 breweries were closed down in the 1960s; in the first half of the 1970s another twenty-two were added to that list, leaving only 155 operating breweries (since 1975 new breweries have opened rather more frequently than old ones have been shut down, so that the number has increased slightly). The 155 breweries were owned by a mere 87 companies, compared with 358 owned by 247 companies in 1960. The market share of the seven national companies, including Guinness, had increased from 45 per cent in 1960 to 75 per cent in 1972 and 80 per cent two years later. The number of pubs owned by the Big Six increased from 16,600 in 1960 to about 40,000 in 1974. During this period the Big Six were involved in 101 takeovers, involving a total of 105 companies which ceased to trade as independent entities.

These are the cold facts of the decline and fall of the independent brewery in Britain. An analysis of the position in individual towns and cities presents an even starker portrait of the erosion of choice and the dominance of the major brewers. Few cities are worse affected than Birmingham, with a population of over a million but until recently with ninety-five per cent of its pubs owned by two national brewers (and the pub swap with Courage, involving only about twenty-five pubs, has had little effect in diluting the duopoly, and in any case has only let a third national brewer share the pickings). Of the twenty-six breweries in Burton-on-Trent in 1869, only five were left a century later, and Truman's closed its Burton brewery in 1971; so four now remain, but the products of one of them (Everard's) can't even be bought in the town. The same story recurs throughout Britain: Morrell's is the only survivor of five twentieth-century Oxford brewers and, even more tellingly, the total of thirty-five brewers in Hertfordshire in 1904 had dwindled to eight by the Second World War and is now down to one, McMullen's.

The reaction to all this of a foreign visitor, particularly one from Bavaria, where there are still over a thousand breweries in operation, would surely be one of incredulity. Yet for the grip of merger mania to have been maintained for more than a decade there must clearly have been economic advantages to be gained by the Big Six. Economists, with their unique ability to produce spectacular theories with little or no relevance to the real world, were quick to produce forecasts for the future of the brewing industry, and predictably they linked size and efficiency in preparing estimates of the 'minimum economic size' of a brewery. Equally predictably, their forecasts have proved to be anything but accurate. The most notorious of the economic studies of brewing was produced by John Vaizey in 1961: *The Brewing Industry 1886–1951: An Economical Study.* He argued that the minimum economic size of a brewery was around 60,000 barrels a year, listing technological innovation, the capacity use of large vessels, and lower materials costs amongst the factors increasing the efficiency of large plants.

It was economic planning of this kind which prompted Watney's to think in terms of supplying the whole of its United Kingdom beer market from four huge breweries, two of them peripheral to the main axis of population; which led Bass Charrington to develop the massive beer factory at Runcorn; above all, which led Whitbread's, despite the cosy family-brewer image, to develop the keg palaces at Luton, Samlesbury and Magor. The advantages of such investment programmes seemed to be transparently obvious, and the

Economists' Advisory Group (commissioned by and reporting to the Big Six-dominated Brewers' Society, it should be added) were adamant that 'mergers have brought economies both in production and distribution.' Incredibly, they were able to conclude that mergers, far from reducing the amount of competition in the industry and the choice available to drinkers, were actually beneficial in allowing national brands to be sold in wider areas.

Anthony Cockerill, too, concluded from his research at the University of Salford that biggest was cheapest, for a number of carefully documented reasons. Predominant is the common notion that efficient plant is large plant, and his figures suggest a sharp gain in economies of scale as output is increased from a low level, with continuing savings up to an output of about one million barrels a year. Cockerill points out that an increase in the capacity of vessels implies an automatic gain in efficiency – doubling the volume should only increase costs by 52 per cent. In respect of distribution and management, he is realistic enough to accept that savings do not appear to be significant. In the field of marketing, Cockerill suggests that 'there is evidence that the major producers can obtain premium prices for their beers, in excess of those available to smaller producers.' This is a quite astonishing statement: the supposed economies of scale having been demonstrated, surely the logical next step is to expect *reduced* prices, it having cost the brewer less to produce his beer, so that the customer can at least derive a price advantage to compensate him for his loss of choice and quality.

Of course, the contradiction in Cockerill's argument comes about because of the fallacy of the economists' prognostications; despite their much-vaunted economies of scale and despite their higher-than-average reliance on high profit margin products (that is to say, low value-for-money products) like keg bitter and lager, the major brewers have failed miserably to compete on price terms with local brewers. The conclusion that the spate of mergers has raised the general level of efficiency and enabled the major brewers to take advantage of changing demands for beer is, at the very least, open to doubt. The brewers themselves have changed the demand for different types of beer through the medium of advertising, which has allowed them to concentrate on keg and lager beers, but the high cost of promoting these products has cancelled out any economies of scale they may have derived, and so they are forced to continue advertising on an exorbitant scale in order to maintain a worthwhile demand for their otherwise unimpressive products.

The Price Commission found that in 1976 the Big Six charged an average wholesale price of 15p per pint for their own beers; the small brewers charged 13p. Marketing, administration and distribution cost over 3p per pint for the big brewers, rather less than 2p for the small brewers, who were unable to obtain the same economies in distribution (although they did not have to transport their beer over ridiculously wide areas) but who did not need to spend much on marketing a superior product. In fact, although the average cost of raw materials was higher for the small brewers, their beer cost twopence a pint less. Furthermore, despite their much higher prices, the Big Six actually contrive to have a *smaller* profit margin than their local competitors. In other words, the existence of the Big Six has worked against the interests of drinkers, who pay higher prices and have less choice, and yet it has not benefited the major brewers themselves, since their profit margins are lower and their prices are higher than either the larger regional brewers or the small brewers.

So the broad picture is one of six major brewers whose policy has been at the same time both aggressive, through brewery takeovers and closures, and defensive, with the acquisition of a huge tied estate which (together with massive advertising campaigns) guarantees sales and also discourages competition from new enterprises. Their policy has been to eradicate beers with low profit margins, such as mild, beers which can present problems with inexperienced or inefficient staff, such as real draught beer, and beers with low volume sales. They have therefore massively reduced the number of brands offered, whilst intensively promoting middle-of-the-road national beers brewed as far as possible to be offensive to no one, but with equally few virtues. And yet such policies have failed to work: locally brewed real draught beers from a small brewery are both cheaper and more profitable than national products. Many factors have combined to create this remarkable situation, although probably the most important has been the rising cost of transport, which has hit firms dependent upon a small number of huge keg factories harder than local brewers supplying compact distribution areas. Also important, though, has been the increasing dissatisfaction of beer drinkers with the products and policies of the big brewers, and it is worth considering a number of the policies which have had adverse effects upon ordinary drinkers.

Such adverse effects include (in no particular order of severity) the closure of breweries and subsequent loss of local beers; the growth of local monopolies as major firms have bought up all their competitors in particular areas; the stranglehold of the tied-house system in such situations; and the closure of pubs, especially in rural areas, and in areas where, because of a local monopoly, the brewers know that customers of pubs that are closed have little choice but to move to another of their pubs, since they own most of the near-by pubs in any case. The case against mergers and the resulting closures of smaller breweries has already been put; it seems futile to argue that in any way they act in the public interest. The loss of the renowned Barnsley bitter has hardly been compensated for with its replacements, namely John Smith's bright beers; no public acclaim followed the withdrawal of Tennant's Queen's bitter and the introduction of bright Trophy in the Sheffield area, and the decision to keg Chester's mild (respectfully known locally as 'fighting mild') from the Whitbread brewery in Salford met with vociferous local disapproval.

Watney's has tried harder than most to soften the impact of the withdrawal of local beers, but this is not to say that its track record is enviable. The case of Tamplin's bitter (to say nothing of the same firm's mild and best mild ales), summarily withdrawn and replaced by Sussex bitter, has been well documented (before long, of course, Sussex bitter was replaced by Watney's Special, and any pretence of pandering to local tastes was discarded: strange, then, that the new regionalization of Watney's should be reversing this trend, with so-called Tamplin's bitter reappearing, though brewed 150 miles from Brighton!). Norwich bitter, too, was a hybrid beer brewed to the requirements of marketing executives wrapped up in the necessity of reducing brands in order to justify large-scale advertising of the select few. The locally popular bitters brewed by Bullard's and Steward & Patteson were withdrawn in favour of the chilled and filtered Norwich bitter, whose sales rest primarily on the monopoly which Watney's has in Norfolk – where the drinker's choice is all too often to go to a Watney's pub or to sit at home. Phipps's draught IPA and pale ale disappeared in the same way with the closure of the Northampton brewery.

This is not to say that all change is to be resisted, and it is certain that some appalling beers existed in 1960: it was, however, possible to avoid them and still find good beer locally. Equally, it is not to say that independent brewers have an unblemished record in maintaining choice. It was bad enough when Samuel Smith's replaced two milds and two bitters with one of each in 1974, but the withdrawal in draught form of the excellent 4X mild after only two years was a disaster. Greenall Whitley, too, showed little tact in the abrupt and unheralded withdrawal of their Warrington-brewed light mild in 1977. Nevertheless, the contraction of choice is essentially linked to the activities of the Big Six, and the flicker of hope induced by the recent introduction of new beers – Fined Bitter, Draught Burton Ale and so on – is small indeed compared with the despair caused by so many brewery closures, with the threat of more to come.

Nettlebed, in south Oxfordshire, has three pubs; all of them are owned by Brakspear's. Local drinkers understandably are not complaining, since all of them serve real draught beer, and the choice of four beers produced at the Henley brewery includes at least two of the highest quality. Most of the pubs in the surrounding villages bear the dark blue signboards of the Henley brewery, but overall (partly because Brakspear's own relatively few pubs) the choice of beers in this part of the country is excellent. Much more sinister is the comparable situation in a place like Bristol, where Courage owned four fifths of the 450 pubs up to 1971. Since then some have been swapped with Watney's, some have been sold privately, and more recently Allied and Bass have gained a foothold through further pub swaps. Yet Courage still owns well over half the pubs in Bristol, with a far higher concentration in some districts of the city; Watney's own seven in ten pubs in Northampton; Ansell's and M & B between them control nine tenths of Birmingham's pubs.

This extreme form of local monopoly is surely indefensible; no brewer has so low an opinion of his products that he needs to exclude all competition. Yet Ansell's and M & B have tried to defend the situation in Birmingham, or at least to deflect criticism. Faced with the comments of a member of CAMRA's national executive that the city was domi-

nated by two breweries offering an abysmal choice of real ale, so that 'if you don't like Ansell's and M & B you stay at home and brew your own', Ansell's retorted that they handled seven draught beers (omitting to state that only two were real draught beers, and even they were only available in cask-conditioned form in a minority of their Birmingham pubs) and M & B's spokesman came up with a mixture of irrelevance and hypocrisy: 'We have 25 different brands of beer, 12 different on draught, 7 of them in traditional casks.' What he failed to say was that only three of the seven cask-conditioned beers were available in Birmingham itself, and that one of these three was introduced to Birmingham pubs (or rather re-introduced) after representations from CAMRA, and was only in half a dozen pubs of the 350 M & B controlled. It is of little use to Birmingham drinkers to know that M & B also has available – but refuses to supply – Springfield bitter, Highgate mild, Worthington bitter and (until recently) Joule's bitter.

The monopoly power exercised by Courage in the county of Avon, which includes Bristol, is worth a closer look, and considerable detail is available since in 1977 CAMRA submitted a report on the monopoly to the Office of Fair Trading, requesting the OFT to hand the case on to the Monopolies Commission for investigation. At that time Courage, through their acquisition in 1961 of Bristol Brewery George's, controlled 613 of the 952 pubs in Avon, or 64 per cent. In Bristol itself, the position was still worse, Courage owning over 69 per cent of the licensed premises. Incredibly, Courage still had this enormous concentration despite the pub swap with Watney's in 1971, when they gained twenty pubs in Northampton and forty in Norwich in return for transferring sixty-eight pubs in and around Bristol to Watney's. The 1971 swap was implemented in the hope that such voluntary measures would deter governmental interference after the publication of the Monopolies

Commission report on the brewing industry in 1969, and it appeared to have worked.

More recently, and perhaps in response to growing criticism from both governmental and independent bodies, the rather larger pub swap with Bass and Allied diluted the Courage concentration in Bristol still further, though Courage still have over half the pubs in Bristol and higher concentrations in some areas. Many of the pubs transferred to Watney's were run-down inner city pubs (some have since been closed) and Courage probably lost very little business while gaining some public approval from a largely cosmetic operation. It is to be hoped that the later exchange will widen choice in a more genuine manner – though it has been simply the substitution of beers from two Big Six companies for those of Courage, and a much more convincing case can be made for freeing the Courage stranglehold by substituting the generally more distinctive beers of local independent breweries.

The demand for such a move is absolutely clear-cut: both drinkers and (in defiance of their employers) Courage landlords have made it clear that they would welcome the chance of greater choice. A petition circulated in Bristol pubs in May 1977 asked for support for the idea of landlords having the option of serving one extra draught beer (other than those supplied by the brewery owning the pub) and in one week more than 12,000 customers signed the petition. Both CAMRA and the local Licensed Victuallers' Association were involved in this exercise, yet Courage's response was that 'our range of beers more than satisfies demands from both licensees and customers.' 12,000 licensees and customers had already proved that statement untrue, yet it was clear that Courage had no intention of letting other beers compete on equal terms in their own pubs. Indeed, a long-standing trading agreement which saw draught Bass in a few of their houses was being quietly phased out. This policy

was being followed despite a Courage spokesman's admission at a press conference that 'the customer does not like our virtual monopoly.'

Even the brewery company themselves recognize this particular local monopoly, then, and they acknowledge local dissatisfaction with the position. But what are the ways in which the monopoly works to the detriment of local drinkers? Predominant among them is absolute power over the market, both over the area as a whole and within Courage pubs themselves. By retaining its tied estate Courage can limit competition to a very small free trade, operating in a tiny number of pubs, and the pubs of rival brewers. In parenthesis it is worth noting that a number of run-down back street pubs, which Courage has been unable to run profitably and has therefore sold, have been transformed into very busy pubs offering oases of choice in the Courage beer desert – and parts of Avon can certainly be a desert for traditional beer, for less than a third of the Courage pubs in Bristol sell real draught beer. The Old Fox in Eastville, bought from Courage by CAMRA's investment company, and the Plume of Feathers in Hotwells Road, closed by Courage and now doing well over twice its previous trade (selling Brain's, Marston's, Samuel Smith's and Wadworth's!) are two examples of previously unprofitable pubs which, freed from the tie to Courage beers, are suddenly prospering.

Within its own pubs in Bristol Courage has restricted the choice both of types of beer and of brands of beer. The type of beer is all too often chilled and filtered beer served by carbon-dioxide pressure, although in areas where competition is more effective Courage has recognized that to sell its beer it needs to offer it in real draught form – in Bath, for example, where the beers available include Devenish, Hall & Woodhouse, Marston's and Wadworth's, amongst others, two thirds of the Courage pubs retain traditional beer, compared with less than a third in Bristol, as noted above. Similarly, the brands of beer available to tied houses have been restricted. As recently as late 1976 Courage was claiming that there was no demand for a strong draught bitter in Avon to complement its two ordinary (very ordinary) cask-conditioned bitters. Yet early in 1977 the free trade was offered Director's bitter, then brewed only in London. Clearly the characterless Bristol-brewed beers had been losing out in the free trade, but where the tied-house system protected them Courage saw no need for an alternative. Only after considerable efforts by Courage landlords did a restricted number of tied pubs get the chance to sell Director's.

The only advantage which the customer could reasonably expect from this monopoly would be lower prices, since the local Courage brewery serves a vast number of pubs in a fairly compact trading area. If anything the reverse seems to be the case, with an emphasis on premium-priced national keg beers and a general level of prices in Bristol which is considerably higher than in parts of the country where there is genuine competition, such as Nottingham and Manchester. The same charge of high prices despite the economic advantages of a high concentration of outlets can be levelled at Watney's in the classic local monopoly area of Norfolk. It has already been indicated that Watney's collected all the Norwich breweries to survive into the 1960s, and then closed all but one of them. The result of these takeovers was that Watney's assumed a position of dominance in twelve out of the thirteen licensing divisions in Norfolk (the unlucky thirteenth is Great Yarmouth, where Lacon's brewery was bought and closed down by Whitbread's).

In the twelve other licensing divisions Watney's control 701, or 64 per cent of the 1,101 full on-licences. Despite the pub swap with Courage, in which over forty pubs in Norwich changed ownership, Watney's still own 65 per cent of the pubs in the city. In the rural areas of the county the position is in many cases even worse, since three-quarters of the villages with one pub have a Watney pub (and many villages which used to have one pub have had it closed – by Watney's). The effects on the drinker of such a concentration of control are in themselves severe; but the monopoly has an even more devastating effect because until 1978 the Norwich Brewery provided Watney's pubs in Norfolk with bright beer only, so that until the last few years, with an increasing interest in real beer from the very small free trade, the county of Norfolk has been possibly the worst in the country in terms of choice and availability of traditional beer. What made the situation (until Norwich Castle bitter was first brewed in 1978) even more frustrating – and commercially incomprehensible – was the recent production in Norwich of real beers for a variety of other regions in the Watney empire. Such products are not available to hard-pressed Watney's licensees in Norfolk, faced with widespread disapproval of the Watney image – which cannot be eradicated by calling the local company by a new name or disguising the pubs – and by intense and increasing competition from the free trade.

Most pubs in Norfolk, therefore, offer Watney's beer, and consequently most offer no real draught beer at all. That is bad enough, and understandably has provoked criticism; what makes the Watney name in East Anglia still less popular is the firm's long-standing policy of closing down and selling off (often with a restriction on future use as a pub) small pubs, normally in rural areas, where such pubs fail to reach set levels of profitability. Pub closures are no doubt inevitable in some cases, but to buy up and close down the local competition, and then to sell pubs de-licensed to prevent future competition is, on the face of it, altogether against any instincts of free enterprise (which brewers usually espouse) and suggests the absolute lack of a social conscience. Smaller brewers normally have the conscience, the local understanding and the integrity to recognize the very severe hardship caused by the loss of rural pubs, and especially the last pub in a village. Christopher Hutt, in *The Death of the English Pub*, quotes the chairman of Adnams as saying that 'A village that loses its pub starts to die. I would never want to be responsible for administering that kind of blow.'

Watney's was presumably convinced that it was justified in the crop of closures which it inflicted upon Norfolk, particularly in the early 1970s: Hutt collected some choice comments, from the trite 'we believe we have a good social conscience and that such decisions are arrived at fairly' through 'we feel the great public benefit (from improving remaining pubs) far outweighs what we are sure is no more than occasional slight inconvenience' to the altogether remarkable claim that the aim of closures is 'to maintain and subsequently improve our service'. It is quite reasonable to wonder whether the villagers of Stiffkey, where there were three pubs belonging to three different breweries (all taken over by Watney's), and where all three pubs have been closed by Watney's, would say the closures had resulted in 'no more than occasional slight inconvenience'. This is by no means an isolated case; since 1966 Watney's have closed twenty-seven pubs in the Downham Market licensing division alone, and three villages (Boughton, which had two pubs, both Watney's, and South Runcton and Wormegay, which both had one pub, owned by Watney's) in that division have been left without a pub.

Decisions such as these are taken so far away from the areas affected that one wonders if the decision-makers have any conception of the role and traditions of a country pub. So many city pubs are virtually indistinguishable from those all around them (especially where the brewers' corporate identity schemes have been let loose on them). Country pubs, though, serve as the focal point of the entire community in many cases, acting as committee rooms for sports clubs, information points for parish organizations, bus shelters and so on. Yet the brewers, hedged in by accountants and their conventional wisdom, appear to have declared war upon the country pub.

Watney's are by no means the only combatants in this war, although they were very early in the field. Courage, in 1975, explained its policy in the Bristol area, where – as with Norfolk and Watney's – a monopoly holding gave it the knowledge that drinkers at the doomed pubs had little choice but to move to another pub serving its beers: ' in many cases brewers have been prepared to retain some country pubs as a social benefit to the community, but this is no longer possible with the rising costs involved ... a number of pubs have been, and will be, offered for sale ... It is inevitable that the majority of pubs affected are in the country.' The language of many such pronouncements suggests that the brewers either don't understand or don't care about the unique character and functions of the country pub; a prime example, to be found in Whitbread's annual report for 1976, states that they are 'implementing our plans for disinvestment' – that is to say, sentencing some villages to a slow death.

Courage sold about 150 pubs in eighteen months in 1975–6, mostly smaller rural pubs which needed modernization of facilities, but didn't do enough trade to justify it. Whitbread got rid of about 250 tied houses in the same period – about three per cent of their tied estate. The Brewers' Society feel that an average year sees a net loss of between 150 and 350 pubs. Costs are rising, and in order to maintain profits at their record levels the brewers are concentrating on their most profitable outlets, and getting what they can from selling the others – so that many smaller communities could soon find themselves without a pub. Ian Breach in the *Guardian* has told the poignant story of a village in Cumbria where there was concern when the real draught beer was replaced by top pressure beer, but within months 'we needn't have worried about the beer. The pub has closed. One of eight to be closed in the same area by the same brewery and with only three weeks' notice, it is now just another of the village's empty buildings.' In the Colne valley in East Anglia the story is just the same: three villages out of seven have been stripped of their pub, Greene King and Whitbread having sold them in the last two years as private houses, a fourth village is likely to join them, and the other three villages, which are all somewhat larger, now have fewer pubs than was the case two years ago.

The real problem, of course, is the tied-house system, since it is the difficulties facing potential free house operators in entering the industry which protects the brewers and makes their policy of pub closures in local monopoly areas feasible. More than three-quarters of Britain's pubs are owned by brewers, and three-quarters of these tied pubs are owned by the Big Six. As the Price Commission found, not only is brewing an extremely highly concentrated industry, but there are substantial barriers to entry because of restrictive licensing laws. The Monopolies Commission reported in 1969 that 'we are of the view that, but for the difficulties of change and transition, a state of affairs in which brewers did not own or control licensed outlets would be preferable to the tied-house system.' The major brewers, of course, would disagree, feeling that since both tenant and brewer have an interest in a pub, both are prepared to improve its services and amenities. 'If breweries ceased to own public houses, there would be an inevitable and rapid decline in standards,' claimed Watney's, which was of the opinion that free houses have a 'low standard of upkeep and generally higher prices'.

But it is not only the brewers who defend the tie. There are those who feel that the survival of at least some of the small brewers depends on the retention of tied houses. Small brewers on average sell about two thirds of their beer through their tied pubs, whereas the Big Six sell half in tied houses, half in the free trade. It has been suggested that some of the least go-ahead, most conservatively organized independent brewers would find it hard to compete with the aggressive marketing of nationally-known products by the big brewers. Controversy rages on this point: others claim that it is the small brewer who has been shown to be most profitable and whose products are most in demand, and that the growing interest in real ale and local beers might give an enormous boost to smaller brewers in an atmosphere of free competition. A more fundamental problem with the destruction of the tied-house system would be that of finding new owners for the pubs, and it might well be that property companies (some almost certainly run by big brewers in any case) would net the bulk of them – which would then certainly be ruthlessly operated on criteria of sales and profitability.

The survival of the British pub, therefore, may well be bound up with that of the tied-house system, but there is no doubt whatsoever that the interests of the drinker would be better served by a more flexible approach. There are a number of possibilities. A gradual improvement could be brought about by the licensing justices, who could refuse to grant further licences to brewers already over-represented in their area; after all, what is the point of the government enacting legislation on local monopolies if the monopolists are free to strengthen their position still further? The justices, too, could have a further role to play in respect of granting new licences, by relating 'local need' (which applicants have to demonstrate) to the need of drinkers for a reasonable degree of choice within a local area. There have been hopeful signs recently that the interpretation of licensing legislation is becoming a little more flexible: in overruling a magistrates' court's decision to refuse a new licence in Newark, a Crown Court judge repudiated the idea that need was all-important, stating that the public interest was of greater significance. He therefore granted the licence, for a free house in a town where all but five of the existing 31 pubs were owned by Courage.

Probably the most realistic method of relaxing the tie, and one which has been shown to have received the support of both drinkers and licensees, is the idea of allowing all tied-house landlords the opportunity of stocking one non-tied draught beer. The massive support from both sides of the bar for the petition in Bristol and its aim of widening choice in Courage tied houses would almost certainly be repeated throughout the country, particularly where local monopolies curtail the freedom of consumers. One could imagine beers from the small Black Country breweries like Holden's and Simpkiss relieving the present gloomy situation in Birmingham; Ruddle's, Charles Wells and others in Northampton; Wadworth's, Arkell's and Donnington in the Whitbread stronghold in Gloucestershire. One could imagine, too, the falling sales of the national brewers, faced with genuine competition from quality products. The likelihood is, therefore, that even this modest relaxation of the tie will be resisted by the Big Six, with their 37,000 tied pubs, for the simple reason that Britain's biggest brewers don't have enough confidence in the standard of their products. Courage has already indicated this with its refusal to consider its licensees' wishes in Bristol.

To summarize, the British brewing industry, through the exceptionally aggressive and acquisitive behaviour of its leading firms, has become remarkably concentrated, with seven firms producing over 80 per cent of the beer brewed in this country, and six of them owning 56 per cent of the pubs, together with having a direct or indirect interest in many more. New firms therefore face considerable barriers to entry. As the Price Commission's report said, 'these are the classic conditions for a monopoly which is likely to operate to the detriment of customers.' There is evidence that monopoly power has been used to reduce choice by closing down breweries and phasing out beers, to eliminate unprofitable outlets despite the social consequences, especially in rural areas, and to manipulate the market through the protective mechanism of the tied-house system.

This monopoly power poses a dramatic threat to the future of real draught beer, despite a continuing and unquestionable demand for the product. Through selective advertising, promoting alternative brews, and at worst a blatant refusal to supply real draught beer, the major brewers can create their own pattern of demand. It is in their interest to move towards a beer market supplied with a small number of nationally advertised, nationally available beers: Whitbread Trophy, advertised for some time as one national beer despite being brewed to different recipes and strengths in most of the company's breweries, is the most bizarre example. It is equally in their interest to promote high-margin beers, particularly lager, which is generally even weaker and less distinctive than their keg bitters, yet is sold at an even higher price. Bright beers and lager offer by far the easiest path for the national brewers, and the revival of real draught beer is an embarrassment which most of them clearly hope is temporary. The future of real draught beer almost certainly lies elsewhere, with the independent brewers. No wonder David Wickett of Sheffield City Polytechnic came to the conclusion that, while the formation of the Big Six might have brought advantages to the big brewers themselves, 'as far as the public interest is concerned, there seems no advantage at all to most people and for many who have suffered a dramatic reduction in choice as well as higher prices the results have been disatrous'.

4 Quality and Choice: Local Brewers and the Real Beer Revival

It is hardly surprising, given the inexorable rise for the Big Six, and their overwhelming marketing power and opportunities to manipulate public taste, that the 1960s and early 1970s saw many of the remaining independent breweries in a mood of despondency. Some of them were undoubtedly resigned to the fate of takeover and closure (having no resources to combat the situation), others felt that their only hope of survival was to ape the big brewers, and only a minority remained determined to stay independent at all costs. Those in the first group, awaiting a takeover bid – and in some cases anticipating events by developing an association with one of the Big Six – must have been depressing breweries to work in. A loss of morale and efficiency would have been inevitable, and this, coupled with an acceptance of declining demand stemming partly from inability to compete with national brands, often resulted in poor beers and apathy on the part of drinkers with no loyalty to an indifferent product.

The charge of poor beer could hardly be levelled at the Yorkshire Clubs Brewery, but the demise of this brewery is a classic case of the gradual decline outlined above. Yorkshire Clubs was one of the final three clubs breweries, and produced an outstanding range of five real draught beers, including the well-liked 6X bitter. By the beginning of the 1970s, however, the brewery was operating at only a quarter of its capacity, largely because it was unable to compete with both its big brother, the Northern Clubs Federation Brewery, and the national brewers, either in terms of advertising or in gaining a tie in clubs by providing loans for installing or modernizing bars. Desperate attempts were made to interest the free trade, but despite being able to offer excellent and low-priced beers, Yorkshire Clubs could interest only a handful of pubs in taking its beer, and in June 1975, Northern Clubs Federation stepped in with a takeover bid. The new owners stated that they saw 'little future for cask beer in the clubs' and indeed by October all brewing at York had ceased and the brewery had become a depot for the Federation's tank, keg and bottled beers.

Even where takeovers were not threatened, some small breweries came to the conclusion that profitable operation was not possible. Melbourn's Brewery in Stamford, for example, ceased brewing in 1974 (but continued to run its pubs, supplied with cask beer from Samuel Smith's) because 'there comes a point when the economic facts must outweigh the ideals of traditional brewing'; parts of the brewery needed modernization, but the volume of business was insufficient to justify such expenditure. Gray's of Chelmsford stopped brewing in the same year, death duties compelling them to sell the site of the brewery. It too became purely a pub-owning company, like a number of firms in the past – the Heavitree brewery in Exeter and the Alnwick Brewery Company providing other instances.

An alternative response on the part of some independent brewers was to adopt the methods used by the national brewers, assuming that processed beers and pressurized dispense would help to ensure their survival. An additional problem for those who followed this course of action is that the swing back to real draught beer cannot easily be accommodated: a good deal of capital (and, for that matter, pride) is tied up in plant for chilling, filtering, pasteurizing and carbonating their beer. It is not surprising, therefore, that Everard's, having made the decision to discontinue traditional beer in the early 1970s, were extremely cautious in reintroducing it: the first 'real' beer was a high-gravity bitter introduced in 1975 which was pressure-dispensed in most of the few pubs where it was on sale! Only in 1977 were more encouraging steps taken, with all four of Everard's beers being served traditionally in one pub initially. A little earlier Paine's which, by the early 1970s, used top pressure in all twenty-four of its pubs, had reverted to traditional dispense in a small number of them. There are still 'bright' breweries who have yet to show signs of reversing their decision, Mansfield Brewery being the most notable example. Others, such as Workington Brewery, have since been taken over (and in Workington's case, resold and converted to a lager factory, which is perhaps a salutary lesson).

Given the policies of the Big Six and the lack of confidence of many of the independent brewers at the end of the 1960s, it seemed unlikely that real draught beer had *any* future. On the other hand, a number of small breweries was absolutely determined to survive: the belligerent determination of Young's of Wandsworth has already been illustrated, and the chairman of Morland's provided another example in his report for 1968 by insisting that 'there is a future for the country brewery . . . smaller breweries operating efficient outlets in limited areas could better serve the public.' Admittedly, this fierce protection of independence was not always successful against the might of the big brewers; the sorry tale of the demise of Cobb's Margate brewery was related in Chapter 3. But there were glimmers of hope, such as that provided in a report by the stockbrokers Sheppard & Chase in 1971, who felt that 'despite the decline in the number of small brewing companies in recent years it is unlikely that such companies will be completely eliminated by takeover or through forces of competition.' Survival, they felt, would come through low transport costs resulting from localized distribution areas, through simple and personal management structures, through local knowledge, and through the development of specialized services such as Davenport's 'beer at home' service.

Although the outbreak of merger mania which was the dominant theme of the brewing industry during the 1960s had reached its climax in 1967–8, it was by no means a spent force when that report was written. The previous year, however, had seen a victory of enormous importance for all those who believed in the survival of independent firms, with the desperate but successful fight against an unwanted takeover bid waged by Boddington's, the renowned Manchester brewers. All the ingredients were there: a Big Six predator in the form of Allied Breweries, anxious for more outlets in the Manchester area, but already with a north-western brewery (Tetley Walker at Warrington), so that no long-term commitment to Boddington's Strangeways brewery could be envisaged. Tetley's beers were more expensive than Boddington's, and certainly not as highly regarded; at that time, too, they were less and less likely to be served in traditional form. Boddington's, on the other hand, brewed four traditional draught beers, always available in unpressurized form, and these four brews together accounted for well over ninety per cent of the draught beer produced at Strangeways – lager taking a mere eight per cent. The firm had a reputation both for giving value for money, and for the quality of its beers, especially the pale but subtly flavoured bitter.

The approach from Allied Breweries towards the end of 1969 was therefore unwelcome in Boddington's boardroom and bitterly resented in their pubs. Boddington's problem, though, was that the board of directors held only about ten or twelve per cent of the shares, whereas Allied had about a quarter and Whitbread (almost inevitably) and Britannic Assurance also had sizeable stakes. The firm's future, then, lay in the hands of its two substantial 'neutral' shareholders and the very large number of small shareholders. Allied's formal offer, announced in January 1970, valued the company at £3,800,000. Boddington's immediately rejected the offer, describing it as inadequate and pointing out that something more than financial gain was at stake: it asked its shareholders to turn Allied down on the grounds that competition between local beers would be diminished and that a popular low-price beer would be eliminated.

By the beginning of February Allied had increased its own stake to almost 30 per cent, but had failed to attract sufficient support from other shareholders, and so it announced a second bid valuing Boddington's at £4,500,000 – considerably more than the brewery's stock market valuation, but a reflection of Allied's determination not to lose face. After all, none of the big brewers had been thwarted, at least since the Second World War, in so public a battle for the control of a major independent brewery company. Whitbread were doubtless aware of this fact, but more significantly it had no wish to allow a major rival to gain a substantial foothold in Greater Manchester, and it therefore backed Boddington's bid for independence. Financial logic alone should surely have tempted most of the smaller shareholders to accept Allied's revised offer; yet they accepted Boddington's advice, rejected Allied and thus ensured the survival of the company as a separate entity. Allied accepted defeat in mid-February, sold its shareholding somewhat later, and have since been visibly reluctant to re-enter the takeover arena.

Boddington's customers have reason to be delighted at the outcome of the battle; one of the thousands of them who wrote in support of the company during the takeover bid is quoted by Christopher Hutt in *The Death of the English Pub*: 'My observation is that these bids are very seldom beneficial to the customer. For instance, some of the brews on sale today are little more than sweetened water, and so far as keg beers are concerned, I regard it as a public fraud.' Boddington's brews no keg beers, lager accounts for a mere eight per cent of its sales, and its real draught beers are still distinctive, still low-priced, and even more enormously popular, in the most highly competitive area in Britain.

Its shareholders, too, can hardly complain at the recent performance of Boddington's: pre-tax profits have risen every year since 1969, from less than £400,000 then to a spectacular £2,906,000 in 1976. Sales of its real draught beers rose by 25 per cent in 1976, and 1977 saw a similar trend; production capacity was increased to 6,500 barrels a week. Production has increased threefold since the bid was fought off, and the growth in sales is entirely due to the quality of the real draught beers it produces – and in particular its bitter, which accounts for three out of four pints brewed. Even so growth in the free trade had to be slightly curtailed because of what chairman Ewart Boddington described as 'some strain on production' resulting from the massive demand for their beers. By 1975 he was saying, 'In my wildest dreams I never thought that we would get on as we have. We are at such a pitch that there is no stopping us now.'

But one thing *could* stop Boddington's despite its buoyant confidence and the family-run nature of the business. That, of course, would be the interest of Whitbread in trying to succeed where Allied failed. Such a development would undoubtedly be just as unpopular with Boddington's and with its customers as the original bid proved to be. But the unpalatable fact has to be faced that, since Allied pulled out, Whitbread – effectively Boddington's saviours in 1970 – have increased their shareholding to around 26 per cent. Should the impetus of Boddington's extraordinary expansion be lost, it has to be borne in mind that Whitbread is in a far better position to make a bid than Allied was in 1969.

In view of Whitbread's recent downturn in trade in the north-west, which has caused the firm some concern, it could well decide to do just that.

The other independent brewery to have survived an overt takeover bid is Jennings of Cockermouth, whose superb beers are widely available in west Cumbria. The predator here was Mount Charlotte Investments, a hotel and catering company which succeeded in collecting the Workington Brewery in 1973, and was clearly attracted by what it saw as the benefits of rationalization resulting from combining the operations of two companies with overlapping trading areas. Mount Charlotte's bid for Jennings (made simultaneously with that for Workington) failed, however, because of the determination of all concerned with the brewery to retain its independence: the initial offer in April 1973 was rejected by the board and, crucially, by the shareholders, and an increased offer the following month was also flatly rejected, largely, it seems, because of Mount Charlotte's plans to close down the Castle Brewery at Cockermouth. The final offer lapsed at three o'clock in the afternoon of 25 May 1973, and the fire siren at the brewery was sounded at the moment of victory as a celebration of Jennings' continuing independence.

At the same time as these remarkable demonstrations of faith in locally brewed and independently produced beers were taking place, a handful of the smaller breweries were recognizing both the increasing disaffection of the public with the national keg beers and their producers, and also, and more importantly, the opportunity to promote on a large scale a truly different and high-quality product. First into this field were two purveyors of very strong and distinctive real draught beers: Ruddle's and Theakston's. By the end of the 1960s Theakston's were brewing at about one third of the capacity of their Masham brewery, producing eighty barrels a week for their seventeen tied houses in north

Yorkshire and Cleveland. In 1968, a new generation of Theakston's took control, and began vigorously marketing Old Peculier, a strong dark beer ideally placed to capture imaginations jaded by a surfeit of indistinguishable national beers. Named after the peculier of Masham – ecclesiastical jargon for the fact that the village of Masham was at one time exempt from the control of the local diocese – Old Peculier had the necessary ingredients of strength, nostalgia and identity to spearhead Theakston's drive into the free trade.

Within the next five years Theakston's expanded their distribution area until it was virtually national and increased production almost to the capacity of the Masham brewery. Yet demand was still rising, and in 1974 the firm took their most ambitious step, purchasing the old State Management Scheme brewery in Carlisle for a mere £90,000 and thereby increasing their production capacity by 1,500 barrels a week at a stroke. All production of draught bitter was eventually moved to Carlisle, with Old Peculier and mild still brewed at Masham. Theakston's beers can now be found virtually throughout the country, from western Scotland to Kent. Success, though, has brought its problems and Paul Theakston was admitting early in 1976 that expansion was so rapid that the difficulty was to broaden the firm's base while retaining family control. Later in 1976 two outsiders joined Theakston's board, and at that time they controlled over a third of the shares between them. The tied houses have been whittled away, too, seven being sold in 1975, and a further six since then, presumably to help finance the Carlisle operation.

The difficulties faced by Ruddle's, on the other hand, have been caused largely by the speed of their expansion from a country brewery with around forty pubs to a major supplier of the free trade and of supermarkets – expansion in 1976, for instance, was so great that there was no spare capacity left for brewing Rutland barley wine on draught. The cornerstone of the expansion has been Ruddle's County, an outstanding strong draught bitter whose success seems to have encouraged the introduction of a number of other beers of similar original gravity – Everard's Old Original, Wells Fargo and St Austell Hicks Special being examples. County now accounts for 65 per cent of Ruddle's real draught production, and this is the beer which is in the vast majority of their two hundred or so free trade outlets, which include quite a number of British Rail station bars.

The brewery's capacity was almost doubled in 1975, from 600 to around 1,100 barrels a week, at a time when potential free trade outlets were literally having to be turned away. Five new fermenting vessels were installed at that time – yet by mid-1976 demand was again outstripping supply and Ruddle's even considered buying another brewery before deciding to expand still further at Langham, investing £1 million in additional brewing and fermenting vessels to bring capacity up to 2,000 barrels a week. The emphasis, though, is still on high-quality beers and traditional methods of production, and Tony Ruddle, chairman and managing director, emphasized that Whitbread's former stake could not lead to a takeover bid: 'We are totally safe from takeover. More than 50 per cent of the shares are owned by the family. The other aspect of our survival is linked to producing a quality product that drinkers want.'

Ruddle's and Theakston's are probably the two names which would spring to mind when tracing the early progress of the real draught beer revival. Others, however, played a similarly important part. Young's, for example, with its ebulliently independent image, built up a fiercely loyal following for their beers in London, where their pubs have become more and more crowded as drinkers have used their feet to avoid national brewers' pubs. Young's special bitter became almost a cult beer in the late 1960s and early 1970s.

Fuller's, its London rivals, also developed a new image and began to promote its Extra Special Bitter as other brewers began to compete for the lucrative London free trade. Further north, Samuel Smith's was recognizing the potential of the free trade and adjusting its image – revising its range of beers in 1974 and promoting Old Brewery bitter, which can be found nowadays in free houses in most of England and Wales; unlike Theakston's, Smith's has retained and even increased its tied estate of around 300 pubs.

These pioneering efforts on the part of a number of independent brewers were in no way hindered by the coincidental activities of a number of publicists, together with the first awakenings of consumer action. Frank Baillie's *Beer Drinkers' Companion* appeared in 1973 and was complemented by Christopher Hutt's *The Death of the English Pub*, which was uncompromisingly critical in its treatment of the activities of the big brewers. Somewhat after the ball had started rolling Richard Boston's Saturday column in the *Guardian* gave it some added impetus. But it was the customer whose reaction was the most unexpected and, ultimately, effective. The Society for the Preservation of Beers from the Wood, founded in the late 1960s and still with us, was never aggressive enough nor sufficiently organized to achieve a lasting effect. But the formation of CAMRA in 1971 has had enormous repercussions and may yet have a permanent effect upon the structure of the industry and its attitude to true public demand.

Founded in a bar in western Ireland during the summer of 1971, the Campaign for the Revitalization of Ale, as it was then called, had done little more than survive by the end of 1972, with very few members and even fewer well-defined objectives (a preference for the word 'ale' as opposed to 'beer', and a recognition that the declining quality of beer could be traced at least partly to the increasing use of carbon-dioxide dispense, were the apparent driving forces).

Before the end of 1972, however, a monthly newspaper called *What's Brewing* had been launched, and the first steps towards establishing a nation-wide network of branches had been taken. The creation of the branch network was probably the most important factor behind the astonishing growth which the campaign witnessed in the next two years; by the time of the annual meeting in March 1973 (which adopted the present title of Campaign for Real Ale) CAMRA had about 1,400 members, a year later there were over 10,000, and by the end of 1975 CAMRA had about 20,000 members, since when the number has remained at roughly that level. Around 140 branches run the campaign locally, an unpaid national executive of twelve members coordinates national activity, and there is a full-time staff of eight. The scale of activity has forced CAMRA to become a limited company, and has also seen the creation of a separate but closely associated investment company which runs a chain of free houses offering a range of real draught beer.

The administrative side of things came very much second in the early days, when the object was to attract publicity for what was then quite reasonably portrayed as a rearguard action in defence of a fast-disappearing product. The object proved enormously successful, in promoting the beers of independent brewers who recognized the demand for real beer, but especially in publicizing the ominous policies of the big brewers. Marches were held in Stone, Staffordshire, and in Barnsley to protest at brewery closures, but it was the Watney group which provided the focus for CAMRA's attacks. The success of such attacks was clearly acknowledged in the poignant statement from Maxwell Joseph which blamed a word-of-mouth campaign for Watney's poor profit performance.

The first reaction of the major brewers, not unnaturally, was to fight fire with fire, and they talked of 'the unedifying spectacle ... when CAMRA, vociferously denigrating other brews, tries to push its pet likes and dislikes down other people's throats' – blatantly ignoring the fact that it was the Big Six which had spent more than a decade phasing out real beers and pushing keg beer down the reluctant throats of a public which had now, just in time, and rather inconveniently for the brewers, started to protest. By the end of 1975, as the Big Six themselves began to increase the availability of their real beers – and, indeed, to launch new traditional beers, a possibility which would have been laughed out of court at the end of the 1960s – their tone had become conciliatory, and a whole batch of policies aimed at rationalization, standardization, and mediocrity had been discarded. One newspaper saw CAMRA's Covent Garden beer festival in 1975 as signalling 'the transformation of what once looked like just another lost cause into a triumphant one'.

By now, however, with the survival of real beer apparently assured, CAMRA had widened its objectives and begun to assume a crucial role as a representative of the consumer in wider matters relating to the brewing industry. There are signs that it has had as telling an effect in this sphere as in the earlier battle for real beer itself, although inevitably less publicity has been associated with these activities. The submission of evidence to the Food Standards Committee was obviously influential in weighting the report towards a stance which was highly critical of the brewers' reluctance to divulge information, and which recommended regulations enforcing the proper labelling of draught beers in terms of type, strength and method of dispense. CAMRA's submission to the Price Commission, too, was clearly of influence in shaping a report which reinforced views the campaign had been stating for years: that the activities of the major brewers had benefited neither themselves nor their customers, and that the smaller brewers offered lower prices, quality products and at the same time a better profit performance. And the series of local monopoly submissions referred to the Office of Fair Trading has led to questioning of the validity of the tied-house system, and to an atmosphere in which the major brewers have hastily devised pub swaps in an effort to ward off government action in diluting monopolies.

The enormous interest in real draught beer created by these achievements induced a climate in which independent firms with high-quality products were in a very strong position: they were in no sense associated with the feelings of resentment aroused by the big brewers and yet they could offer traditional draught beers to a free trade which (especially in southern England) was suddenly eager to counter the declining interest in national keg bitters by stocking a range of real beers, some of which quickly built up formidable reputations. All their advertising suddenly became 'real' and 'traditional' too. Young's and Arkell's issued lists telling us where to find 'real draught beer' (though at that time Arkell's still used pressure in the vast majority of their outlets!); Morrell's advertised its 'tradition of fine draught beer'; Eldridge Pope introduced 'Royal Oak real ale, a tradition in brewing revived by Huntsman ales'; Shepherd Neame promoted its 'traditional draught beer from the heart of the hop country'; Marston's even told us that 'real beer drinkers love it'.

The changing fortunes of the drinker in search of a decent pint of beer are well illustrated by the case of Dorset. Four independent breweries survive in the county, but all of them could advance a number of valid reasons for the low proportion of their pubs which sold real beer in the early 1970s. Dorset is a sparsely populated county (except for south-east Dorset, which includes Bournemouth and Poole) and there are consequently a great many rural pubs with a very low turnover, which therefore have difficulty in keeping traditional beer in good condition. Equally, as a holiday area, demand is seasonal, and may only be sustained at a viable level for real beer for a short summer season. Again, nationally promoted beers are at an advantage where tourists, divorced from their distinctive local brews, may drink bland, characterless, national beers in preference to local beers which they do not know, and which may be brewed for a very different palate. Top pressure was therefore the rule rather than the exception with Devenish, Eldridge Pope, Hall & Woodhouse and Palmer's.

Palmer's, the smallest of the four Dorset brewers, have given no visible signs of a change of policy, which is a pity in view of the excellence of their IPA in unpressurized form. The other three, though, have all taken steps to improve the situation, while retaining top pressure in most pubs. Devenish, alarmed at the results of a CAMRA survey which revealed that its beers were among the weakest in the country, increased the strength of its two bitters, and renamed the stronger one Wessex best bitter. At the same time it began to increase the number of its pubs selling unpressurized beer, although these remained in the minority, and its publicity emphasized the difference between traditionally-dispensed and pressurized beer, listing the Devenish pubs according to the method they used. Hall & Woodhouse, too, began in 1976 to implement a policy of installing handpumps in appropriate pubs, and its excellent best bitter began to appear much more commonly in real draught form in both the free and the tied trade.

Eldridge Pope, however, caught the imagination to a greater degree by launching a new real draught beer, Royal Oak, which was to be served *entirely* in real draught form, and then only by licensees who attended a training course and passed an examination relating to the care of the beer. Royal Oak, with an original gravity of 1048, was re-created from a recipe last used in October 1896, and was launched in October 1975. Initially there were thirty outlets for the beer, a superb malty, strong bitter, but the number of outlets taking Royal Oak increased fivefold in two years and it is now available in an area stretching from the south coast to near Cheltenham, and from London to south Devon. Less encouraging, though, is the fact that Eldridge Pope's Dorchester bitter and IPA are rather less widely available in draught form, and sadly there are few signs that the number of their pubs selling real draught beer will increase dramatically from the present fifty or sixty – about a third of the tied estate. Nevertheless, given the major constraints of small rural pubs often without adequate cellars, the independent Dorset brewers have contributed significantly to the increased availability of real beer which has been the feature of recent years.

In many ways the smaller brewers, whose senior personnel are rather closer to the details of production and distribution, are in a strong position to ensure the quality of their product. Ruddle's, for example, quickly recognized the problems which might occur as the result of large temperature fluctuations on long journeys; its answer was to buy a refrigerated dray to make the journeys to and from London. Similarly, Eldridge Pope foresaw problems with intermediate loading and unloading of casks at its depot in Taunton, and developed a container system in which beer is trunked from Dorchester to Taunton and stored unopened in temperature-controlled containers at the depot until local crews deliver it, opening the container for the first time when it reaches the pub it is destined for. Again, smaller brewers can spend more time on individual problems, and the licensee has more confidence that his problems will be dealt with if the voice at the end of the phone is that of senior management rather than an answering machine.

All this simply emphasizes the attention to detail and to quality which many independent brewers have recognized as essential in a very competitive market. Some such brewers have found the competition strong enough to compel them to alter their policies fundamentally. Gibbs Mew, for example, having abandoned cask beer altogether in the 1960s and brought out no less than three keg bitters, was stranded by the upsurge in demand for traditional draught beer, which meant that an entire sector of the free trade was closed to them and at the mercy of neighbouring suppliers such as Wadworth's and the Dorset brewers. Inevitably, a reversion to real beer had to come, and 1976 saw the introduction of Bishop's Tipple, a barley wine usually served from casks on the bar, though sometimes by handpump. In the following year premium bitter was marketed (actually it was a perfectly standard bitter), and the Silver Jubilee saw Gibbs become one of the few brewers to celebrate by brewing Jubilee bitter, their third real draught beer.

Everard's, as we have seen, also regretted their decision to phase out traditional beer – it now publicly admits that it was a mistake – and after the initial experiment with Old Original in 1976, it test-marketed its full range of four beers on handpump in the Globe on Silver Street, Leicester, a superbly renovated Victorian town pub. The test was an outstanding success, and the number of outlets with real beer began to increase quickly, a measure of Everard's new commitment being its order for casks worth £75,000. Many other local and regional brewers were at this time increasing either the range of their real beers, or their availability, or both. Bateman's added XXXB, a strong bitter, to its two excellent established cask-conditioned beers, Holden's began to brew its special bitter, and Hook Norton introduced Old Hookey, a unique and fairly potent old ale.

This activity should not be allowed to obscure the efforts of the minority of brewers whose commitment to traditional methods and naturally-stored and served beers had never wavered. The list of brewers who make real ale available in every one of their tied houses is not over-long, but reads like something akin to a roll of honour, and includes some of the most respected brews and brewers: in alphabetical order, Adnam's, Batham's, Boddington's, Brain, Greenall Whitley (Wem), Hartley's, Holt, Hook Norton, Hyde's, Okell's, Timothy Taylor, Yates & Jackson and Young. Their reasons for retaining traditional draught beer to the extent that they have may vary from inability to raise the capital necessary to install equipment for processed beers, to sheer faith in a distinctive product, though inertia must have played a role. But the fact remains that without some of these brewers, and others such as Jennings, Ridley's, Robinson's and Thwaites, which pressurize the beer in only a tiny minority of their pubs, the quality and choice of real ale currently available would be much reduced, and the impetus for its protection might be correspondingly weaker.

In whatever way the revival of interest in traditional draught beer is measured – increased sales, soaring turnover, higher profits, spectacular returns on capital employed, and so on – the message over recent years has been clear. Local and regional brewers are more efficient, more profitable and more popular than the major brewers. This state of affairs has prompted, for the first time since 1904 (with the exception of clubs breweries), new firms to enter an industry which is characteristically, and quite reasonably, portrayed as impossible to break into, given the monopoly power which exists and the virtual stranglehold of the tied-house system. The entry of new firms is an encouraging sign that changes in the structure of the industry, such as those generated by the disposal of pubs which the Big Six find unprofitable to operate, may lead to greater choice in the future as more outlets become free of the tie. Great credit, though, must go to the enterprises which have pioneered this small-scale but welcome invasion.

First, though, mention must be made of a firm which not so much entered as re-entered the brewing industry. Selby

Brewery stopped brewing at its north Yorkshire brewery in 1954, largely for economic reasons; in particular, because of the small scale of production, the firm was unable to justify much-needed expenditure on new equipment. Selby negotiated an agreement with Dutton's to bottle Guinness for it, while selling Dutton's beers in Selby pubs. In 1964 the pubs themselves were sold to Dutton's and the firm concentrated on its bottling activities. In 1972, however, the brewery reopened, largely as a result of the initiative of Martin Sykes, a relative of the owners and a real-ale enthusiast, who 'felt that there is still a demand in the trade for real beer, rather than for the coloured water with bubbles in that is now generally available.' A strong bitter was brewed and made available to the free trade, and one tied house was acquired, at Howden in north Humberside. Despite various changes of brew, the renaissance has continued, and two real draught beers are produced, together with a naturally-conditioned bottled pale ale specially brewed for one pub, the Brahms & Liszt in Leeds.

Not all of the new enterprises have recognized the need to produce traditional draught beer – or at least they have a different definition of the product than that widely accepted. Bill Urquhart, for instance, head brewer at Watney's Northampton brewery – the old Phipps brewery – was made redundant at the age of 58 when Watney's closed down the brewery. His reaction was to set up a brewery in an eighteenth-century barn at his home in the village of Litchborough. He had already become disillusioned with the sameness and lack of character of keg bitter – even the keg which he brewed himself for Watney's – and with the way in which breweries were run: 'It had got to the stage in the industry where we were brewing by committee. The market research men said what they wanted, then the accountants and everyone else.'

Litchborough Brewery's Northamptonshire bitter, therefore, provided a chance to return to creative brewing. It was, however, filtered before being racked into casks and was dispensed by top pressure in the first few outlets, because although Bill Urquhart acknowledged that the sentiments of the real beer movement were right, he felt that 'they are wrong on a lot of the technicalities.' Production hovered around three barrels a week for the first few months (compared with up to 12,000 barrels a week that he had been brewing for Watney's) and casks of unfiltered beer are now available. The £2,000 spent on wort kettles, a cooler, fermenting vessels and so on has proved to be a very worthwhile investment.

Purists find less to argue about with Pollard & Co. at Stockport, understandably so, since the driving force behind David Pollard's entry into the brewing industry was a disenchantment with the big brewers and their methods which had been fostered by a series of takeovers affecting companies he had been a brewer for – the last being Threlfall's in Salford in 1967. A year after Whitbread had acquired Threlfall's, David Pollard left, feeling a strikingly similar sense of frustration to that expressed by Bill Urquhart: 'I felt the incentive had gone out of the window. The accountants and engineers had started running things. All the big firms wanted were pasteurized, carbonated beers with no taste or character.'

David Pollard's answer was to convert part of a disused cotton mill at Reddish near Stockport into a brewery, where he started to produce John Barleycorn bitter in the spring of 1975 (he had been running his home brew shop in Stockport since leaving Threlfall's). Initial output was seven barrels (250 gallons) a week of his bitter, which had a relatively high original gravity of 1044. Plans for a dark mild brewed at about 1037 have yet to materialize, however. The brewery cost more than £5,000 to equip, mostly with utensils which had to be adapted to serve a new purpose, and with expenditure on casks and so on something like £20,000 was needed before the brewery began operations. John Barleycorn bitter was brewed from an all-malt recipe with no sugar added, and was quickly successful in local free houses, the first being the CAMRA Investments pub in Hyde, the White Gates, where deliveries were at first made on a milk wagon owned by a local farmer.

Within two years output had increased to thirty-five barrels a week, and six free houses in Greater Manchester and Cheshire were taking the beer, together with a pub in Devon which, not surprisingly, had to make special arrangements for deliveries. The original gravity of the bitter had been reduced to 1036, partly because of customer reaction ('people used to say the taste was all right but they complained it was too heavy') but primarily because of the need to compete on price with brewers like Boddington's, who were also pushing for free trade outlets. Indeed, the strong competition in the north-west for a limited free trade forced David Pollard to consider expansion in other areas, notably southern England, which offered more scope and higher prices, more free outlets and a greater readiness to accept and indeed to seek out the more esoteric brews.

1977 saw plans to open a Pollard's tied house too – Polly's, on the corner of Princess Street and George Street in the centre of Manchester. The intention was to serve a range of real draught beers, with due emphasis on John Barleycorn bitter, but above all to provide an element of stability in terms of outlets for his beer, given that the north-west's free trade was unpredictable and in some cases effectively tied to one of the established brewers in the area. Nevertheless, the spread of Pollard's into the free trade continued, into pubs such as the Windmill at Whiteley Green, near Macclesfield. Judged purely in commercial terms, the achievement of Pollard's in establishing a successful business in the most fiercely competitive area in the country has been outstanding, and his plans for future expansion are perhaps the most exciting of the new brewing concerns.

The Penrhos Court brewery project, on the other hand, has to be seen in the wider context of the conservation of an outstanding group of medieval and later buildings; the brewery is seen partly as a means of ensuring the survival of part of the Court complex by introducing a new use for some of the buildings. Penrhos Court, a mile or so east of Kington in Herefordshire, consists of an early cruck house with a variety of outbuildings, which enclose three sides of a quadrangle around a central cobbled area and a duck-pond. The earliest parts date from around 1280, and include features of a regional style of carpentry of which only a few examples survive, all in a small area in the Welsh Borders. This cruck house was added to in the fourteenth century and again in Elizabethan times. By 1970 the house was on the verge of collapse, however, and seventeenth-century barns were already falling apart. In 1972 Martin Griffiths bought the Court and began the Penrhos Preservation Project, aimed at rescuing the buildings by finding a new use for each of them. The first step was to convert one of the barns into a restaurant specializing in local and regional dishes. The second, in conjunction with Monty Python star Terry Jones and Richard Boston, was to re-build a tall barn to provide space for the Penrhos Brewery.

Herefordshire (like Rutland, a county which refuses to die) is the second largest hop-producing county in England, and yet its long tradition of brewing was eliminated completely in the twentieth century. Kington alone had four home brew pubs within living memory – the Castle Hotel, Railway Tavern, Sun and Wine Vaults. Penrhos Brewery, though, is the only operating brewery in the county, largely because of a series of mergers which has given Whitbread the lion's share of the county's pubs. The brewery was designed by Peter Austin, formerly head brewer at Hull

Brewery, and is cleverly constructed in three storeys of the tall barn, with fermentation taking place in another barn near by. Malt from East Anglia, milled on the premises, local Hereford hops, and spring water are the ingredients of four different beers. Within a matter of months brewing was taking place three times a week, 180 gallons being produced each time. Already there was talk of a larger mash tun and more fermenting vessels being required.

The first two beers were bitter, a subtly flavoured and quite strong beer with an original gravity of 1042, and Jones's Ale, a unique 1050 beer which is brewed using very few hops in an attempt to re-create something of the old flavour of 'ale'. The latter brew was initially available at only two outlets, one of them the Crown at Aymestrey, near Leominster, whereas Penrhos bitter was quickly to be found in ten or twelve pubs within a fairly wide radius. Unlike Pollard's, who found entry into the free trade sometimes difficult, licensees actually asked Penrhos for the beer, and the difficulty was to restrict trade to an area sufficiently close to the brewery to make deliveries economic. Some further expansion, especially in Hereford, is envisaged, but 'the intention is to produce a small amount of first-class beer for local consumption.'

By the time Penrhos bitter was available in local pubs a number of other brewery projects were under way; indeed some had already reached fruition. Nigel Fitzhugh had begun to brew fourteen barrels a week of his Blackawton bitter in part of a small disused smithy in the village of Blackawton, near Dartmouth in south Devon. The capacity of his brewery was about forty barrels a week, and demand from local free houses suggested that his cask-conditioned beer, though brewed from malt extract, might soon be produced in that sort of quantity. Much more ambitious were the plans of Norman and Alan Rutherford, whose West Crown Brewery in a converted maltings in Newark-upon-

Trent had a capacity of about 500 barrels a week, and who envisaged selling their beer in as many as 100 outlets. West Crown's Regal bitter, brewed from barley malt and hops with no adjuncts, and racked into wooden casks, was brewed three times a week by the end of 1977 and sent to free-trade outlets as far apart as south Yorkshire and the Home Counties.

The lucrative London market naturally attracted proposals for new breweries, and three schemes surfaced in 1977 alone. The most ambitious, perhaps, was the Covent Garden Community Association's plan to revive brewing in part of the building in Covent Garden which once housed Combe & Underwood's brewery, one of the largest in London in the nineteenth century. An alternative use for the site appears to have been preferred, however, and the scheme is in abeyance. Godson's brewery, in a disused warehouse in Clapton, is very much in existence, though, producing the very light Anchor bitter for a number of pubs in the capital. Formed by Patrick Fitzpatrick, it is an extension of Godson's beer wholesaling business, and is the first new London brewery this century. The plans of Alan Greenwood, who built up a chain of real ale off-licences, suffered a number of setbacks, and his Straightsmouth Brewery – the new name for the former Lovibond's brewery in Greenwich, which stopped brewing in 1960 – now looks unlikely to start brewing again. But the trickle of new ventures shows signs of becoming a flood as free houses recognize the sales potential of new and often distinctive real draught beers.

Probably the most encouraging aspect of the renewed interest in real draught beer has been the apparent reversal of the slow trend towards the complete disappearance of the tradition of home-brew pubs. Most seasoned drinkers can recall a number of such pubs which have ceased to produce their own beer in the relatively recent past – the Britannia in Pinfold Gate, Loughborough, which still advertises home-brewed beers on the gable end of the building, the Exeter Arms in Derby, and the Blue Bell at Hockley Heath, in Warwickshire, now a cider house, are representative examples.

The Black Country in particular is full of pubs advertising home brew in faded lettering on outside walls, or in old pub windows. For almost a decade, though, the number still producing home-brewed beer stood at four: the Blue Anchor at Helston in Cornwall and three pubs in the west Midlands, the Three Tuns at Bishop's Castle in Shropshire, the All Nations at Madeley, now part of Telford New Town, and the Old Swan at Netherton, near Dudley, the only surviving home-brew pub in the Black Country.

A major problem for home-brew pubs is the change of ownership: advancing years on the part of the owner tend to lead to the cessation of brewing, so that the new owner takes on a pub which is no longer actively brewing. Home brewing, too, is an intensely personal activity, and many such brewers have taken the secrets of their craft to the grave rather than pass them on. As an example, George Cooksey followed his father as brewer at the Old Swan not so much because Mrs Pardoe, the pub's celebrated proprietor, selected him (though she might well have done so) as because his father refused to divulge the recipe and his particular brewing technique to anyone else. George Cooksey's son is now learning the trade in preparation for a further generation of Netherton home brew. The Pardoes, too, are determined to keep the pubs (the other one is the White Swan, a modern pub near Dudley town centre) in the family, and thus preserve a Black Country tradition which, like a number of others, is on the brink of extinction.

The death in 1975 of Bill Lewis, husband of Eliza Lewis, who has carried out the brewing at the All Nations, Madeley, for over forty years, appeared to threaten the future of the home brew there, but fortunately Mrs Lewis's determination, coupled with the decision of her son Keith to give up his job in Southampton to return to Madeley and prepare to take over the pub and the brewing, seems to have secured the future of the unique light mild which is brewed behind the pub, situated in a pleasant backwater near the Blist's Hill open air museum and the Severn Gorge at Ironbridge. Similarly, the decision of John Roberts, licensee and brewer at the Three Tuns in the tiny market town of Bishop's Castle, to retire in 1976 also caused fears for the closure of the brewery, with its capacity of only about twenty-four barrels a week. Fortunately a buyer prepared to continue the tradition of brewing appeared, and Peter Milner – schooled by John Roberts himself – has taken on the pub and ensured the continued production of the superb XXX bitter and dark mild.

The Blue Anchor at Helston has also had to survive a recent change of personnel. Geoffrey Richards retired after forty-two years at the pub as licensee and brewer, but the beer is still brewed between two and four times a week by his son, although the new licensee is Shirley Jones, a native of Helston. Three different draught beers are brewed, an extraordinary degree of choice for a small brewery with a capacity of 100 gallons per brew. The beers are an ordinary bitter, a strong medium bitter, and special bitter, which has an original gravity of 1053 degrees and is therefore one of the strongest bitters in Britain. And one of the regulars at the Blue Anchor is Geoffrey Richards, who still lives close to the brewery in Helston.

The survival of these four long-established home-brew pubs has been complemented recently by the emergence of a number of others, although some of the newcomers are content to serve pressurized beer or to use adjuncts, rather than to emulate the four survivors, whose commitment to real draught beer is total. The Mason Arms in west Oxfordshire was the first to enter the fray, with a bitter produced from malt extract but dispensed by handpump. The Fighting

Cocks, near Grantham in Lincolnshire, uses handpumps, too – but to pump up a home-brewed bitter which is stored under a layer of carbon dioxide in bulk tanks in the pub's cellar. The Miskin Arms in mid-Glamorgan serves only pressurized beer, too, and the New Fermor Arms at Rufford in Lancashire, despite attempts to take into account the wishes of its customers, also stores the home-brewed bitter and dark mild under pressure in tanks.

Somehow one gets the feeling of an opportunity missed with some of these pubs; not so, however, with the John Thompson at Ingleby a few miles from Burton-on-Trent. The landlord – the pub is named after him – installed a miniature brewery complete with mash tun to avoid the need for malt extract, which often leaves the beer with a cloying palate, and now brews John Thompson Special XXX bitter, with a gravity of 1045, so successfully that it sells comfortably more than any of the other beers on sale in the pub. Two other home-brewing ventures should also be mentioned: the Miners' Arms, a restaurant at Priddy in Somerset, where the naturally-conditioned bottled Own Ale is available with meals only, and Traquair House, close to Innerleithen in Peebles-shire, where Peter Maxwell Stuart, twentieth Laird of Traquair, stumbled upon a disused brewhouse in 1965 and now produces the exquisite and very strong Traquair House Ale in equipment which includes a copper dating from 1739 and 200-year-old oak fermenting vessels. Most of the output is pasteurized and bottled at Belhaven Brewery, but at Traquair itself naturally-conditioned bottled beer is on sale, and very rarely a cask of the ale on draught can be found.

The new mood amongst drinkers and independent brewers was contagious. More and more independent brewers either committed themselves to the production of real draught beer where they had previously been wavering – Wadworth's, for example, started to re-convert the minority of their pubs that had been converted to top pressure – or reintroduced cask-conditioned beer after a period of keg-only or bright-only production, as with Everard's, Gibbs Mew or Paine's. Many such brewers enjoyed an enormous expansion into the free trade, which was saturated with national keg beers suffering from declining demand, and which was now clamouring for distinctive and high-quality real draught products. New brewery companies, mostly small-scale but sometimes with impressive plans for expansion, were beginning to enter the market.

The Big Six, surveying all this, had two main options. One was to put all their faith in lager, which was the fastest-growing section of the trade but which was coming under fire with charges of over-pricing, and about which there were contrasting opinions on future growth. The other was to promote their real beers, and in some cases to introduce new ones (whilst, in most cases, still ploughing ahead with plans for increasing their lager capacity).

Watney's, as ever, threw itself energetically into a new style of operation. Recognizing the policies that had led to the hugely successful campaign against it – corporate identity, standardization, rationalization, and centralization – it adopted almost the opposite policies. Pubs which had received 'the treatment', in particular involving new white lettering on a red background, were treated again, this time in a variety of styles and in any colour except red. No brewer's name could be found outside these pubs, as a curious bout of corporate lack of confidence set in. Centralization, too, was reversed, and no less than nine regional brewery companies were set up, including, as we have seen, the quaintly named Mann's Northampton Brewery Company, a regional company without a brewery in a town where Mann's had no historical connections whatsoever. Standardization was replaced by a rash of new beers, led by Fined Bitter in the south-east and East Midlands, but including

Mann's bitter, Tamplin's bitter, Truman's Tap bitter, and a new bitter from Wilson's.

Ind Coope's Draught Burton Ale, introduced progressively in the second half of 1976 and now in several hundred pubs in south-east England and parts of the Midlands, provided a major boost for real draught beer because of the sheer scale of Ind Coope's investment in the new ale – an indication that although lager remained Allied's major growth area, they accepted the declining market for keg, and thus the future of the group's cask-conditioned beers was at least partially assured. The market for strong draught bitters in the London area was quite obviously the target, as brewers fought to emulate the success of Young's special bitter and, in a much more limited number of outlets, Fuller's strong bitter. Courage Director's bitter, at one time on the verge of extinction, became much more readily available, often, like most of these beers, at a premium price. The original gravity of draught Bass was increased amid a fanfare of publicity to give Bass Charrington an entrant in this lucrative market.

Whitbread and Scottish & Newcastle, however, have remained intransigent despite their rivals' preoccupation with real beer, albeit in some cases as a short-term sop to drinkers' demands. Whitbread, in particular, seems hell-bent on a policy of catering primarily for the demand for lager, and it clearly has faith in the most optimistic forecasts for such demand. S & N have toyed with the idea of real beer in a few bars in Glasgow, Edinburgh and London while supplying bright beer to north-east England and pinning its hopes on new lagers.

Even Whitbread, however, appear to have tacitly accepted that the day of premium keg bitters is over, and its advertising promotes the hybrid Trophy, part real draught and part bright, and brewed to a dozen or more recipes, instead of Tankard. Lager and bright beers, indeed, seem to have replaced keg as the chief threat now, with brewers such as Courage, while promoting Director's bitter in the short term, pressing on with the construction of the Berkshire Brewery, a bright beer factory near Reading which doomed Simonds's brewery to certain closure and threatens Courage's London, Bristol and Plymouth breweries in the longer term.

It would be unwise, therefore, to place too much faith in the Big Six as suppliers of real beer. The independent brewers, to repeat what has been said, are better placed to cater for what now seems certain to be a lasting demand. This is not to say, however, that the future of some of these independent brewers, and therefore of part of the current wide choice of real draught beers in most parts of the country, is necessarily assured. There are a variety of problems facing independent breweries, and it is as well to consider some of these in order to recognize the forces still at work which, directly or indirectly, threaten the beer drinkers' heritage. It is, after all, only a few years since Melbourn's and Gray's were forced to cease brewing, and although the present climate of opinion almost certainly rules out opposed takeover bids by the Big Six, outside firms have forced their way into the industry and this process does not as yet appear to have been completed.

The first 'outsider' to acquire a local brewery company was Northern Dairies (since renamed Northern Foods), which acquired a 27 per cent shareholding in Hull Brewery towards the end of 1971, when Allied and Bass sold their stakes in Hull; at that time it was said that Northern Dairies had 'no plans apparently to build this up to a controlling interest'. By April 1972 it had been successful in a bid for the remainder of the shares. In 1976 Northern Foods acquired 12 per cent of Tolly Cobbold's shares and the speculation was that a further takeover bid had been submitted, although Tolly's managing director was adamant that 'the philosophy of this company is to remain independent', pointing out that the families held a substantial proportion of the shares. The following year Ellerman Lines acquired Tolly, leaving a disappointed Northern Foods spokesman to claim that the price paid was 'ungenerous'.

Ellerman had already entered the brewing industry with its acquisition of Cameron's, the Hartlepool brewers, three years earlier. There were historical links here and the takeover appears to have worked well, with Cameron's left very much to its own devices. But with the Tolly board of directors in such a strong position, its sudden decision to accept a takeover seems more curious. Patrick Cobbold's explanation was that 'the future looked a little difficult on our own due to trends in trading.' Such a bland statement ignores the tremendous success of other local and regional brewers – yet there is some truth in it, for compared with pre-tax profit margins of 19 per cent earned by Boddington's and 10 per cent by Young's (and these are representative rather than exceptional) Tolly achieved only 5 per cent in 1976. A second reason advanced was that it would prevent a takeover by a national brewer – yet the likelihood of this was negligible, given that a bid would almost certainly attract the interest of the Monopolies Commission.

Ellerman, then, have over 1,000 pubs and two very widely separated breweries and trading areas. Northern Foods have just one brewery and some 230 tied houses. Inevitably there must be fears that these two firms, and quite possibly certain others, will be interested in extending their brewing interests (indeed, Northern Foods made an unsuccessful bid for Shipstone's in 1978) and, in Ellerman's case, buying further in order to fill the gap between West Hartlepool and Ipswich. According to one observer, 'Ellerman has approached Greenall Whitley and received only a gentle rebuff.' Other companies which, for this and other reasons, tend to excite the stock market are Wolverhampton & Dudley Breweries, Davenport's and Burtonwood. A further possibility to be entertained is that of defensive mergers between the larger independent brewers in order to ward off unwelcome approaches – and it has been suggested that Greenall Whitley and Wolverhampton & Dudley have held discussions in the past. The implication is that the activities of outsiders such as Ellerman and Northern Foods are likely, directly or indirectly, to lead to further mergers, and the lesson from the past is that this can only mean less choice.

Despite the likely disapproval of the Monopolies Commission towards bids for local brewers from the Big Six, their shareholdings in some independents must give cause for concern, and in any case an uncontested bid for a company which decides not to fight a takeover, or is in no position to do so, is another matter. Rumours of suspected bids are notoriously unreliable, but Morland's, for instance, have had to deny receiving approaches from Whitbread in the recent past, and there are other companies where Whitbread's shareholding is uncomfortably large. Equally, Bass Charrington's 30 per cent stake in Maclay's is ominous. Further concentration of pubs and power into the hands of the Big Six certainly should not be ruled out, however socially undesirable it may be.

Probably the most difficult problem for the family-controlled brewers is that of capital transfer tax, which imposes a tax burden on lifetime gifts and on share transfers on death. Inevitably controversy rages on the merits and demerits of the tax, but what is not open to differing interpretations is the catastrophic effect which capital transfer tax as originally implemented would have on some of the smaller brewers. The effect would certainly be more damaging than that of death duties – and these alone were a sufficient reason for Gray's of Chelmsford to be forced to stop brewing and sell the brewery site. The essence of the problem is that brewing is a capital-intensive industry, and even the smallest brewer has capital assets far in excess of exemption levels which have been enacted or proposed in order to exclude small businesses from liability. The Brewers' Society is of the opinion that the tax 'could mean that within a decade many of the breweries at present privately owned could be put out of business by having to sell up to meet the tax.' The society drew up a list of fifty-one breweries which could be affected in this way. Roger Barker, a director of Mitchell's of Lancaster, has equally clear-cut views: 'It is impossible for the ownership of these firms to stay in a family.'

One positive step which can be taken by independent brewers is to organize themselves so as to make both take-overs and tax problems less likely. Young's of Wandsworth, for instance, has a profit-sharing scheme which now holds over fifteen per cent of the share capital, and other brewers, such as Eldridge Pope, have also taken steps to encourage employees to become shareholders. Adnams, too, launched a capital reorganization scheme to protect the company against the threat of a possible takeover and against the problems caused by capital transfer tax. Other small breweries, however, have less confidence in the future and either because of the indifference of the younger generation of a family, or the lack of enthusiasm of the older generation in making arrangements to maintain family – or independent – control, they may cease to exist in the foreseeable future.

Such pessimism, however, should not be allowed to conceal the fact that the smaller brewers are no longer in headlong retreat, and more than that, the best of them are now selling their beer aggressively and successfully in competition with national keg beers which at one time seemed likely to sweep real draught beer out of British pubs. One comme
tator observed in 1964 that 'at the present ti
brewing industry is as active as the yea
fermenters.' The reference there
merger mania, but the stat
difference being that t

establishment of new breweries and the promotion of new real draught beers. For the first time in decades, the measure of choice available to the drinking public is increasing.

This is true both of the number of breweries and of the number of real beers they offer. Brewers are re-discovering the advantages of offering a strong bitter, and Bateman's, Eldridge Pope, Holden's, Ind Coope and Paine's are just some of the companies to have introduced them. Similarly, old ale and winter brews are suddenly increasing in popularity; Hyde's Anvil strong ale and Wethered's Winter Royal are recent additions to the range. We are unlikely to see a return to the days when breweries offered as many as a dozen different qualities of beer, but some of the smaller breweries shame their larger rivals by producing an impressive range. Taylor's, for example, brews six different beers at its brewery in Keighley, Wadworth's gives the drinker a choice of four different bitters, and Morrell's offers two milds, two bitters, and two strong ales (though in many cases such as these the full range is not, of course, often available in the same pub). The continuing decline of mild, despite campaigns aimed at preserving the extra measure of choice which it represents, seems to be inevitable, and a number of milds has been discontinued recently, but it seems fair to say that such losses have been more than balanced by the plethora of new beers.

The slowing down of takeover activity is the central reason for this continuing degree of choice. As John Young scathingly says of mergers, 'using whatever euphemism may be thought appropriate these changes are called "greater use of assets", "rationalization", "response to change", etc., c. but the only certain thing is a further reduction in the swe of beers. Local brews enjoying great popularity are Not an in the name of a mythical god called progress.' dient be least for the time being. The second ingre- simply the al of the independent brewers has been d interest in the public bar in what goes on in the industry. It is no longer enough to advertise a product on television or to have a national identity to be able to sell millions of pints of a mediocre product. Not before time, there has been a renewed demand for quality beers, and a growing realization that mass promotion and slick marketing on the pub counter cannot hide a lack of taste and an excess of gas in the glass.

One past chairman of the Brewers' Society said during his term of office that 'one thing is certain, you must not treat the electorate, however dense they may appear to be, as inferior beings.' The major brewers, in a sense, made exactly that mistake; as a result they found themselves faced by a drinkers' revolution, led by the Campaign for Real Ale, but with the support of a vast number of drinkers who found that British beer and British pubs were changing in a way that was convenient for the brewers but totally against the drinker's interests. The revolution is far from over, but it has started to change brewers' attitudes and may yet succeed in saving a part of our heritage. To give the last word to John Young, 'Thankfully the British public are at last resisting these changes ... Good luck to them, they'll need it.'

5 The Beer List: A Guide to the Real Beer Breweries of Britain

Against all the odds, real draught beer has not only survived but is increasingly widely available in many parts of the country. Even more surprisingly, considering the continuing brewery closures and withdrawal of draught beer perpetrated by the Big Six, the number of breweries and real beers has actually increased in recent years. Nevertheless, areas remain where real beer is a rarity, and real beers continue to be brewed which, even at their best, are insipid and characterless. It is the purpose of this chapter to guide real beer drinkers by listing all the breweries in Britain which produce real draught beer (the minority that doesn't is simply omitted), commenting upon the beers that they produce, their availability in real draught form, the number and location of the brewery's tied houses, and any involvement in the free trade.

The surviving breweries are by no means evenly spread across the country; there are particular concentrations in and around Manchester and the West Midlands conurbation. Some rural areas also have more than their fair share – Dorset, for example, has four independent breweries, and there are four breweries in neighbouring Wiltshire. Conversely, there are only three independent breweries in the whole of Scotland – Maclay's of Alloa (in which Bass Charrington has an ominously large shareholding), Belhaven Brewery on the east coast, and the home-brew house at Traquair. Cask-conditioned beers are also available from Lorimer's (a subsidiary of Vaux), Younger's, McEwan's, and in minute quantities from Tennent's Edinburgh brewery. Nevertheless, real ale is the exception rather than the rule in Scotland, and much of the cask-conditioned beer is in any case served by systems using air pressure, which certainly doesn't enhance its quality.

South-bound travellers will find little improvement in the north-east of England, where Scottish & Newcastle is the dominant force. Tank and keg beers are also the rule from the Northern Clubs Federation brewery and Vaux of Sunderland, though the latter's Sunderland draught bitter might possibly herald a change of heart. Cameron's remains the best bet for real beer enthusiasts. The situation in north-west England is very different. Cumbria has excellent ale from both Jennings and Hartley's; Mitchell's and Yates & Jackson brew in Lancaster. These four companies supply real ale to all but five of the 237 pubs they own between them. Matthew Brown's record is not so good, but its Blackburn neighbour Thwaites is firmly committed to real draught beer. Greater Manchester has no less than eight breweries producing real draught beer (see map 1) and Boddington's, Holts, Hyde's and Lees send real draught beer to all their pubs (Lees to all Greater Manchester pubs, but not to some further afield), Robinson's to all but one, and Pollard's to all their free-trade outlets. With substantial quantities from Higson's, Burtonwood, Greenall Whitley and Tetley's, too, the north-west is extremely fortunate.

The West Midlands has a further concentration of worthwhile breweries (see map 1), including three very small breweries in the Black Country (the celebrated Batham's, together with Simpkiss and Holden's) and five home brew pubs – the Three Tuns, All Nations, Old Swan, Old Washford Mill and John Thompson. Banks's and Hanson's, Mitchell's & Butler's (with breweries at Wolverhampton, Walsall and Cape Hill), Ansell's, and Davenport's are the larger brewers in the area, together with Marston's, Everard's, Bass and Ind Coope in the brewing capital of Burton-on-Trent. Real beer is readily available in the West Midlands; in the east the supply is rather more patchy, though the best patch is undoubtedly Nottingham, with excellent and cheap ales from Hardy & Hanson's, Home Brewery and especially Shipstone's. Hoskins in Leicestershire has only one tied house, while the reluctant Leicestershire brewery (it insists that Rutland still exists) of Ruddle's has reduced its number of tied houses to just one whilst building up a very extensive free trade.

East Anglia includes the beer desert of Norfolk, together with Adnam's country in east Suffolk, Ridley's excellent beers around Chelmsford and the two major brewers in the area, Greene King and Tolly Cobbold, both of which serve real draught beers in only about a quarter of their pubs. There has been a dramatic increase recently in the number of breweries in London, though Young's still leads the way by providing real ale to all of its tied houses. Outside breweries from as far away as Yorkshire (Samuel Smith's and Theakston's), Wiltshire, Dorset and south Wales are as important as any of the other London brewers as suppliers of traditional beer – though Ind Coope have reintroduced it in many pubs and Charrington's still supply a large number of houses with its bland IPA.

The south-east has Fremlin's (only occasionally real draught) and Shepherd Neame in Kent; Harvey's and the superb King & Barnes in Sussex; and the equally good Gale's in west Sussex and Hampshire, where Brickwood's beers from Portsmouth are popular. Dorset has Hall & Woodhouse, which has shown an increasing commitment to traditional draught beer recently; Devenish and Eldridge Pope, both of which have taken encouraging steps but still pressurize the beer in the majority of their pubs; and Palmer's. Wadworth's beers, brewed in Devizes, are well known in most of the West Country, as to a lesser extent are Arkell's.

Two outstanding Cotswold breweries are Donnington, near Stow-on-the-Wold, with seventeen superb rural pubs, and Hook Norton, the Oxfordshire brewery with thirty-four tied houses. Morrell's, Morland's and Brakspear's complete the list of Oxfordshire brewers.

South Wales has a number of excellent cask-conditioned beers from its surviving breweries, notably Brain's, a firmly traditional brewery in the centre of Cardiff. Real beer is also fairly common in pubs served by Welsh Brewers (part of Bass Charrington), Felinfoel Brewery and Buckley's. The South Wales Clubs Brewery also supplies real draught beer to a good number of clubs and to a number of free houses, especially in the Bristol area. The new Penrhos Brewery is a further source of traditional draught beer for south-east Wales and the Border Counties.

Such a whistle-stop tour of the country cannot do more than whet the appetite; the rest of this chapter attempts to fill in the details in as concise a form as possible. The layout of the chapter is straightforward. Breweries are split into three levels of operation: the home-brew pubs, the local and regional independent brewers, and the national brewers – the Big Six together with Guinness. Breweries falling into each of these categories are listed alphabetically under the name most commonly used to describe them (although there are some cross-references where two names are equally well-known, such as Henley Brewery and Brakspear's). Technical terms are avoided wherever possible; the number in brackets which follows the name of each beer is the original gravity of that beer, as defined in Chapter 1. Comments on the beers are inevitably subjective, though every one is based upon personal experience; drinkers can use them as a reference point for their own sampling exercises.

The Home-brew Pubs

Many of the recent additions to the list of home-brew pubs have chosen to produce beer which does not conform to the definition of real draught beer given in Chapter 1: the beer is either stored under carbon-dioxide pressure, or pressure-dispensed, or both. Such pubs find no place in the list in this chapter. The four surviving old-established home-brew pubs (All Nations, Blue Anchor, Old Swan and Three Tuns) have, however, been joined by six new home brewers, although only three of these produce draught beer on a regular basis.

The beer brewed at the *All Nations* in Coalport Road, Madeley (now part of Telford New Town in Shropshire), is a palatable light mild (1032) brewed by Eliza Lewis with the help of her son Keith. Mrs Lewis has been brewing at the All Nations for over forty years – having helped her father with the brewing at the Bird in Hand in Ironbridge before that – and brews once a week in a building behind the pub which houses a mash tun and copper, a cooling vat and a fermenting vessel. The All Nations itself is a plain, homely pub near the Severn Gorge, close to the Blist's Hill museum of the Industrial Revolution.

The *Blue Anchor* in Coinagehall Street, Helston, Cornwall, is another of the scattered survivors of the home-brewing tradition. The Blue Anchor itself dates from the fifteenth century, and has been in the hands of the Richards family for over a hundred years. Geoffrey Richards was the third generation of the family to brew here, producing three different strengths of beer for sale only at the Blue Anchor itself. Mr Richards retired in 1975 after forty-two years as the brewer and licensee, but the beer is still brewed two or three times a week by his son for the new licensee, Shirley Jones. The three beers are an unusual ordinary bitter (1033), a powerful and distinctive medium bitter (1050) and special bitter (1053), the second strongest bitter brewed in Britain, and a fine, heavy, yeasty brew.

A very recent addition to the beers available in the West Midlands is the brew produced at the *John Thompson* pub in Ingleby, a small village east of Burton-on-Trent. The brewery is the brainchild of John Thompson, the licensee, and it produces XXX special bitter (1045), an excellent strong, well-hopped bitter. The beer is brewed in a miniature version of a traditional brewery, complete with mash tun to avoid having to use malt extract and thereby run the risk of making an inferior beer; and it is produced from crushed pale malt, hops and water, together with a strain of yeast from Marston's. The beer is all dry-hopped, too, to give a characteristically bitter flavour. The pub, a converted farmhouse, is the only outlet for the beer, and is well worth a visit.

The *Mason Arms* at South Leigh, near Witney in Oxfordshire, is another recent addition to the list of home-brew pubs, Donald Litt having started to brew there in 1975. The initial output was 72 gallons a week, and at one time some of the beer was bottled by Donnington Brewery, but demand soon reached the point where all the beer was needed for sale on draught. The beer is a fairly dark bitter (1040) with a malty taste, available only at the Mason Arms.

The *Miners' Arms* is solely a restaurant, and the home brew there can be consumed only with meals; furthermore, it is available only in bottled form. Own Ale (1048), a naturally-conditioned pale ale, was first brewed in 1974 by Paul Leyton, a former rocket scientist turned restaurateur, and at first there were plans to sell it on draught in local free houses. Nothing seems to have come of these plans, though, so that a meal at the restaurant near Priddy in Somerset is necessary for drinkers wishing to sample the beer.

The *Old Swan* – Mrs Pardoe's – in the centre of Netherton, right in the heart of the Black Country, is probably the most famous of the home-brew pubs. Sole survivor of more than 200 home-brew pubs in the Dudley area alone, it is a superb, friendly Black Country pub with a weighing machine, ancient stove, enamelled ceiling and magnificent bank of handpumps in the public bar, and a late Victorian elegance in the smoke room. The Pardoes moved here in 1932, though the pub had been brewing its own beer long before that, and Doris Pardoe now runs two pubs (the White Swan in Swancote Street, Dudley is the other one, although there is not always enough home brew to keep two pubs supplied and so the White Swan also has Springfield bitter and Hanson's mild and bitter) and a number of off-licences. The brewer, George Cooksey, followed his father into the job, and has been brewing at the Old Swan for more than twenty years. The home brew (1034) is a light mild which has some of the characteristics of a bitter, but which is never less than good, and at its best is a superb, malty beer. It may not be consistent, but it is wonderfully good value and a unique experience for beer drinkers – who can be seen crowding the pub at week-ends, to the detriment of its local trade, and, ultimately, of the Old Swan itself. That, though, is the price of success.

The *Old Washford Mill* at Redditch New Town, hasn't the same pedigree as the Old Swan; the home brew here was first produced in 1978. Nevertheless traditional methods and materials are used in the brewery, which is sited in the former restaurant of the pub. The Old Washford Mill is part of a chain of free houses, and it is possible that the beer, a medium-strength bitter called Old Glory (1038), may be available in a number of these pubs. Initial output was planned to be about fifteen barrels a week.

The *Three Tuns*, in the small Welsh Border market town of Bishop's Castle, is the most outwardly impressive of the home-brew pubs, with the brewery buildings across a yard from the pub. Beer has been brewed at the Three Tuns since at least 1642, though the brewhouse dates from 1888; at that time the beer was widely available to other pubs and to private customers in the immediate area. More recently the trade with other pubs has been largely discontinued, although there is one additional outlet for the beer – the Fox and Hounds at Stottesdon, a remote village in southern Shropshire. John Roberts, who was the licensee and brewer at the Three Tuns until 1976, was the third generation of his family to run the business; in 1899 his grandfather was complimented on the quality of his ale by the rector of a near-by village, who had the Bishop due to visit him and said, 'I want them to exclaim with one voice, after they have tasted your beer, "Roberts deserves well of his country as he is the only man who has developed a cure for the agricultural depression!"' Nowadays the beer is brewed by Peter Milner and it is still quite outstanding. There is a malty, satisfying dark mild (1032) and an excellent strong and very pale bitter (1042), which has a very distinctive hop flavour.

The *Traquair House* brewery, near Innerleithen in Peeblesshire, is a superb example of conservation at its most positive, in this case involving the resuscitation, after a break of about two hundred years, of brewing in what is reputed to be the oldest inhabited house in Scotland. The brewhouse and eighteenth-century utensils were discovered in 1965 by the twentieth Laird of Traquair, Peter Maxwell Stuart, and Traquair House Ale was re-created – perhaps not the same Traquair brew as that tasted by Mary Queen of Scots in 1566, but nevertheless a fine, dark, malty strong ale with an impressive original gravity of 1075, which is filled into individually-numbered bottles (64,000 of them in 1976). The majority of the ale is pasteurized at Belhaven Brewery, but ale sold at the house itself is naturally-conditioned, and occasionally a cask of draught Traquair Ale is made available at beer festivals, though with an alcohol content of

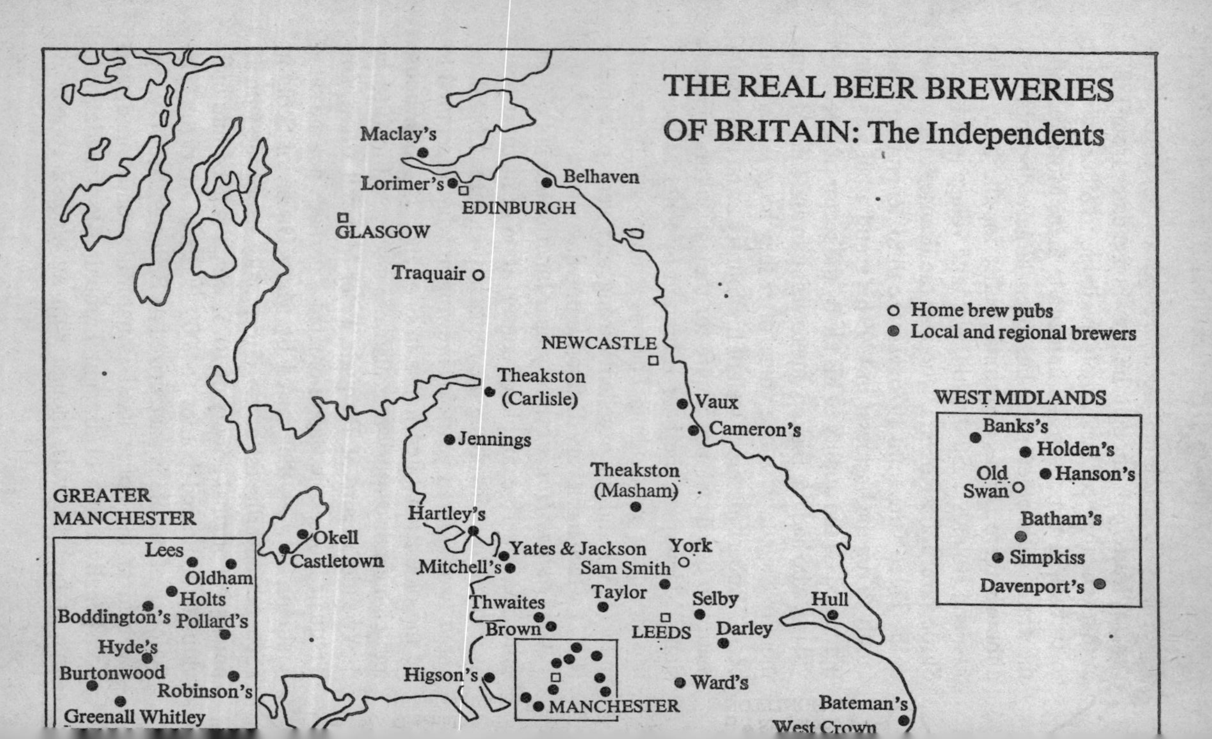
THE REAL BEER BREWERIES
OF BRITAIN: The Independents
Home brew pubs
Local and regional brewers
Maclay's
Lorimer's
EDINBURGH
Belhaven
GLASGOW
Traquair
NEWCASTLE
Theakston
(Carlisle)
Vaux
Cameron's
Jennings
Theakston
(Masham)
Hartley's
Okell
Castletown
Yates & Jackson
Mitchell's
York
Sam Smith
Taylor
Thwaites
Brown
Selby
LEEDS
Darley
Hull
Higson's
MANCHESTER
Ward's
Bateman's
West Crown
WEST MIDLANDS
Banks's
Holden's
Old
Swan
Hanson's
Batham's
Simpkiss
Davenport's
GREATER
MANCHESTER
Lees
Oldham
Holts
Boddington's
Pollard's
Hyde's
Burtonwood
Robinson's
Greenall Whitley

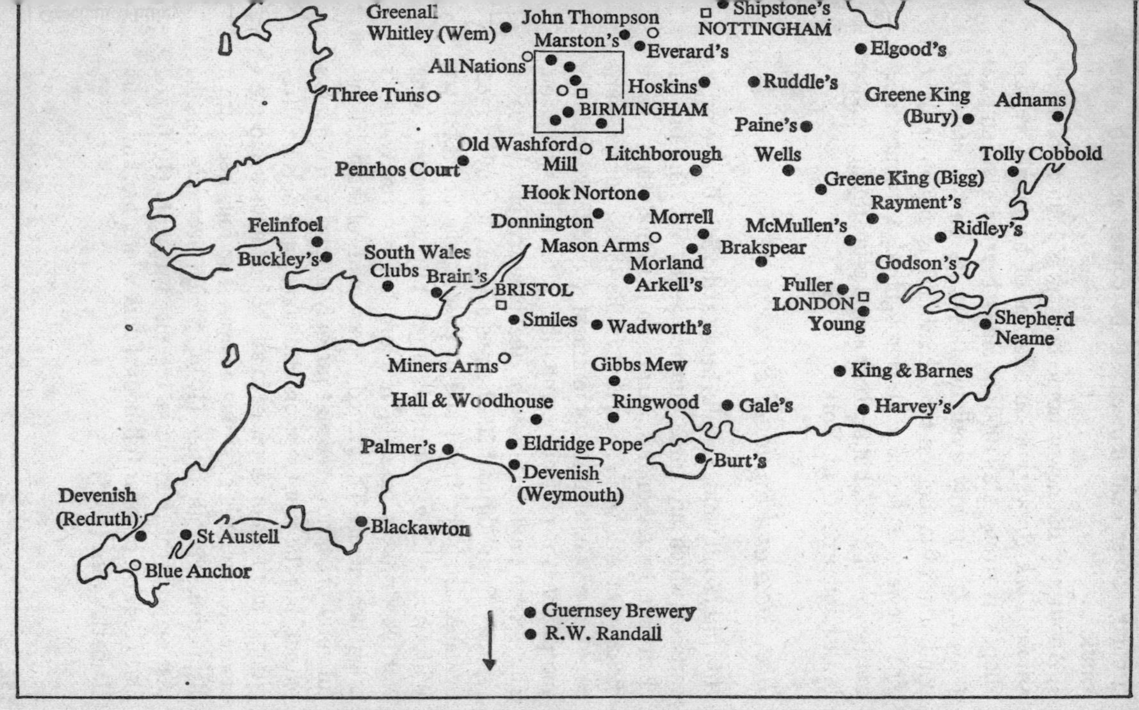
Greenall Whitley (Wem)
John Thompson
Marston's
Everard's
Shipstone's
NOTTINGHAM
Elgood's
All Nations
Three Tuns
Hoskins
BIRMINGHAM
Ruddle's
Greene King (Bury)
Adnams
Paine's
Old Washford Mill
Penrhos Court
Litchborough
Wells
Tolly Cobbold
Greene King (Bigg)
Hook Norton
Rayment's
Donnington
Morrell
McMullen's
Ridley's
Felinfoel
Mason Arms
Brakspear
Buckley's
South Wales Clubs
Brain's
Morland
Arkell's
Godson's
BRISTOL
Fuller
LONDON
Young
Smiles
Wadworth's
Shepherd Neame
Miners Arms
Gibbs Mew
King & Barnes
Hall & Woodhouse
Ringwood
Gale's
Harvey's
Palmer's
Eldridge Pope
Burt's
Devenish (Weymouth)
Devenish (Redruth)
St Austell
Blackawton
Blue Anchor
Guernsey Brewery
R.W. Randall

around 12 per cent it needs to be consumed with some caution.

Another of the newer home brewers is John Boothroyd, whose *York Brewery* is an offshoot of his home brewing shop. His strong ale (1060), a malty beer with an unusual flavour, is normally available in bottles only – naturally conditioned – though on rare occasions it is sold on draught. The brewery is actually at Boroughbridge, twenty miles north-west of York, but the beer is sold primarily at the shop in Bishopthorpe Road, York.

The Local and Regional Brewers

Adnams (Southwold, Suffolk) brews at the Sole Bay brewery, parts of which are three hundred years old. The present chairman, John Adnams, carries on the family name from the days of Adnams & Sergeant in the 1870s, but the company has proved that its commitment to traditional methods and products is perfectly compatible with rapid expansion. The recent modernization of the brewery has increased capacity from 700 to 1,200 barrels a week, largely to meet demands from the free trade in East Anglia and London. With Greene King, Adnams is largely responsible for giving Norfolk drinkers oases of real draught beer in Watney's bright beer desert. The 72 tied houses, many of them delightful rural pubs, now account for only a third of Adnams's output, but the insistence on traditional materials and traditional methods of dispense in all the tied houses and most of the free trade is as strong as ever. The four beers are a distinctive, smooth bitter (1036), which accounts for the vast majority of production, together with mild (1030) and olde (1042), a popular full-bodied dark winter ale, and Tally Ho barley wine (1075).

Anchor Brewery: see Godson's.

Arkell's (Stratton St Margaret, near Swindon), run by the Arkell family since the foundation of the firm in 1843, is an example of a small brewery which reached the conclusion during the 1960s that pressurized and keg beers were sufficient to satisfy their customers. Only three of the 64 tied houses offered real draught beer, even though a misleading leaflet entitled 'real draught beer and where to find it' was issued in 1974. More recently, however, Arkell's has taken much more encouraging initiatives, and around a third of its pubs now stock real beer; it has moved decisively into the free trade, too, sending its beer as far as London; and it has started brewing the dark, strong yet bitter Kingsdown ale (1060) to complement its two bitter beers – John Arkell bitter (1033), named after the founder, and BBB (1038), a well-hopped and pleasant brew.

Banks's (Wolverhampton) and *Hanson's* (Dudley) are the two surviving breweries of the Wolverhampton & Dudley Breweries Ltd, one of the largest of the independent brewers, having grown through takeovers in Lichfield, Shifnal, Kidderminster, Worcester and elsewhere, to gain a strong representation in many parts of the West Midlands. The real stronghold of the company is the Black Country (half the pubs in Dudley sell either Banks's or Hanson's ales) and its excellent and low-priced beer has a devoted local following. The beers are fairly similar, both breweries producing a pale and sweetish bitter (1038) and a comparatively strong medium-dark mild (1035). Mild accounts for about three-quarters of draught beer sales. No keg beers are produced, neither are other brewers' kegs sold in most pubs, and real beer is available in virtually all of the 800 tied houses, occasionally dispensed by handpump but much more commonly by metered electric pump.

Bateman's (Wainfleet All Saints, Lincolnshire) has been renowned for its 'good honest ales' since 1874 – indeed, during its centenary year it claimed that there was no point in producing a special celebration brew because its standard beers were so good. The brewery was founded by the grandfather of the present chairman, and transferred to its present site at Salem Bridge towards the end of the nineteenth century. The beers are an excellent malty bitter (1037), a superb creamy dark mild (1032) which is surely one of the outstanding milds in the country, and the strong XXXB bitter (1048), introduced in 1977 to meet the demand for a heavier beer. Of the 110 Bateman pubs, all in east Lincolnshire and the Fens, 106 serve real draught beer, and there is an expanding free trade, with outposts in Leeds and Cambridge.

Batham's (Brierley Hill) has been brewing at the Delph brewery since 1905, when the premises were acquired from the Worcester Brewing and Malting Company, but the business had been started in Netherton in 1877, and had moved to Cradley Heath in 1900. At one time nineteen pubs were owned, but these have been whittled away as death duties have taken their toll, and there are now only eight, all offering real ale: the Vine (or Bull and Bladder), next to the brewery, the Lamp Tavern at Queen's Cross in Dudley, and others at Pensnett, Kinver, Stourbridge, Kidderminster, Shenstone and Chaddesley Corbett. There are two draught beers: a dark mild (1036) and a superb bitter (1043) with a unique combination of flavours, sweetish but with a dry aftertaste.

Belhaven Brewery (Dunbar, East Lothian) is one of only two in Scotland which have escaped the clutches of the large brewers, and has built up a considerable reputation for the quality of its beers. The brewery was taken over in the early

1970s by Clydesdale Commonwealth Hotels, which has now sold off almost all its other interests and renamed itself the Belhaven Brewery Group. There are only a handful of tied outlets but more than a hundred free-trade accounts, mostly in central Scotland. Allied Breweries has a trading agreement, together with a financial stake in the group, and there are consequent fears for the long-term future of the brewery. The beers are a dark mild called 60/– light (1031), 70/– heavy (1036) and 80/- export (1042), all of which are excellent bitter beers, and strong ale (1070). Regrettably air-pressure dispense, which many feel spoils the palate of the beer by preventing natural carbon dioxide from escaping from the cask, is used in most outlets.

Blackawton Brewery (Blackawton, South Devon) is one of the newest breweries in the country. Nigel Fitzhugh began brewing in part of a converted smithy in 1977, and immediately created a good deal of interest in south Devon free houses, although his Blackawton bitter (1040) is brewed from malt extract. The brewery, largely using equipment from the old Tamar brewery in Plymouth, which Courage closed down in 1975, has a capacity of forty barrels a week.

Boddington's (Manchester) is one of the best-known of the independent brewers, largely because of its resistance to a takeover bid in 1970 from Allied Breweries, a triumph for real draught beer which has already been traced in detail in Chapter 4. Thankfully its range of four traditional draught beers is still widely available in Greater Manchester, Lancashire, Cheshire and parts of north Wales. There are around 280 tied houses (half of them within ten miles of the brewery), every one of them serving traditional draught beer, and there is a fast-growing free trade. The beers are a fairly sweet dark mild (1031), a light mild (1033), a magnificent, really bitter and very pale bitter (1035) and a strong ale (1063).

Border Breweries (Wrexham) is an enigmatic company which had appeared to be promoting real draught beer in the mid-1970s, so that 83 of the 200 or so tied houses offered real beer in 1975. Two years later half of these had been converted to keg, and there were fears that more would follow. It might be prudent to sample the impressive range of draught beers – a nondescript dark mild (1031), the lighter and more delicately flavoured Exhibition mild (1032), the dark and malty best mild (1035), and bitter (1034) – fairly soon. A further problem is that Whitbread has a minority shareholding.

Brain's (Cardiff) has been brewing outstanding beers at the Old Brewery in the heart of Cardiff since before 1882 (when the present company was constituted) and the brewery itself has been in use since 1713. The commitment to traditional brewing methods is total, and all the 100-plus tied houses offer handpumped real draught beer. The beers are dark (1035), which is a subtle yet full-flavoured mild, a pleasant light bitter (1036), and a distinctive malty best bitter called SA (1041). The Crown at Skewen, on the A467 near Neath, also offers MA, a unique mixture of dark and SA. The tied houses are heavily concentrated in the Cardiff area, but there is also some free trade as far away as Bristol.

Brakspear's (Henley-on-Thames) is more commonly known simply as the Henley Brewery, which was founded in 1756 by Hayward & Brakspear. Growth has involved the takeover of breweries in Henley, Wokingham and Goring-on-Thames, but the 130 tied houses are still clustered in a very small area around the brewery, and many of them are unspoilt gems in the Chiltern countryside. There is also free trade, especially in London, but the brewery is now operating virtually at capacity. All but a handful of the pubs sell real draught beer – offering one or more of pale ale (1035), a magnificent ordinary bitter, subtly flavoured and well-hopped, special bitter (1043), which is rather sweeter, an excellent old ale (1043) which is the special bitter with caramel added, and a thin dark mild (1031). All the cask-conditioned beers are dry hopped. Classic Henley Brewery pubs include the Lamb at Satwell, off the B481 south of Nettlebed, the Crooked Billet at Stoke Row, to the east of the A4074, and the Six Bells at Warborough, off the A423 close to Shillingford Bridge.

Brown (Blackburn). Matthew Brown's Lion Ales are widely available in Lancashire and Cumbria, although only a small proportion of Brown's pubs sell real draught beer (there are 600 pubs in all). Brown's takeover of Workington Brewery in 1975 led to the withdrawal of draught beer production there – and the renaming of the plant as the Lakeland Lager Brewery. The choice of real beer has been reduced in the recent past, with the withdrawal of Old Tom, an excellent strong draught ale, and keg beers such as Heritage have been vigorously promoted. There is some indication that the seemingly irreversible trend towards bright beer might have been slowed or even halted, however. Two draught beers are produced: an acceptable bitter (1036) and a dry-flavoured dark mild (1031).

Buckley's (Llanelli) brewery dates from 1767, and the Buckley family is still closely involved with the running of the business. The company is, however, associated with Whitbread, and there have been the inevitable rumours of takeover and closure. Buckley's itself has a large stake in the neighbouring Felinfoel Brewery. There are about 180 tied houses, widely dispersed in south Wales between Swansea and the Dyfed coast, but only about half of them serve traditionally-dispensed beer. Best bitter (1036), a pleasant standard bitter (1031) and a dark sweetish mild (1031) are brewed.

Burt's (Ventnor, Isle of Wight) is one of the smallest surviving brewery companies, with eleven pubs and a small free trade (including, incredibly, London). The Ventnor brewery dates from 1840, although damage in the Second World War necessitated virtual reconstruction, which had been completed by 1951. The three traditional draught beers are VPA (1040), a truly bitter beer, the much thinner LB (1030), and BMA (1030), a fairly light mild. In their unpressurized form Burt's ales are available at the Mill Bay on the Esplanade in Ventnor, one of only two tied houses with real beer, and at a number of free houses, including the incomparable Yelf's bar in Union Street, Ryde.

Burtonwood Brewery (Burtonwood, near Warrington) was established in 1867 by James and Jane Forshaw, whose descendants still run the brewery. Until the 1930s the vast majority of the tied houses were in Lancashire and Cheshire, but since then the company has expanded into north Wales. A continuous programme of modernization in recent years has seen the construction of a new boiler house, fermenting rooms, and, inevitably, kegging facilities. There are about 290 tied houses, most of them with real draught beer – a light, pleasant bitter (1036), a thin but malty light mild (1031), and a dark mild (1032) with a characteristic flavour which is not to everyone's taste.

Cameron's (Hartlepool) was the subject in 1975 of the first venture into the brewing industry by Ellerman Lines, the shipping company which historically had had a sizable stake in the firm. Through taking over brewers in Darlington,

Scarborough, Malton, West Auckland and York, Cameron's has grown to the status of a regional brewer, with some 750 tied houses, most of which serve real draught beer. Considerable changes have been made recently to the range of beers available, although the beautifully balanced bitter (1036) and Strongarm (1041), a rather fuller and sweeter bitter, are well established. Scotch bitter was discontinued in 1975 and replaced by best malt ale, a 1034 brew containing no sugar which was itself unsuccessful and has now been replaced by a new dark mild (1033). Crown Ale (1051), introduced for the Silver Jubilee, may well become a standard brew too.

Castletown Brewery (Castletown, Isle of Man) has the distinction of having been run by a Mr Kegg – yet it is subject to the Manx Pure Beer Act, which restricts the raw materials of Manx-brewed beer to malt, hops, water and yeast. Real draught beer is available in all but one of the thirty or so tied outlets, dispensed either by handpump or direct from the cask. There is a very pleasant, well-hopped bitter (1036) and a curious light mild (1036), both beers being brewed from the same basic recipe. Bass Charrington has a substantial shareholding, so much so that Castletown actually brews Jubilee stout, but the firm appears anxious to remain independent and to maintain its policy of offering high-quality real beer.

Crown Brewery: see South Wales Clubs.

Darley's (Thorne) is an enigmatic firm which has shunned publicity in recent years and, despite the fact that it produces distinctive real beers, seems determined to push bright beers at the expense of its traditional products. Founded in the mid-nineteenth century and family-run until 1978, Darley's brew an IPA (1035) which many consider to be an acquired taste, a light mild (1032) and a more widely available dark mild (1032). Mild is by no means in all of the 100 tied pubs, and the IPA is often in bright form in the larger town pubs in Yorkshire and Humberside. Acquired by Vaux in 1978.

Davenport's (Birmingham) is probably more famous for its 'beer at home' delivery service, which reaches a quarter of a million customers between Yorkshire and the West Country, than for its real draught beers. This is understandable, since real beer is available in less than half of its pubs, and since the policy in newer and renovated houses is to store the beer under a blanket of carbon dioxide. Yet it accepts that the publicity surrounding CAMRA has given it a boost: 'it certainly can't have done us any harm,' according to its marketing director. But less than half of the 115 tied houses offer real draught beer – the excellent, well-hopped bitter (1038) and a less distinguished dark mild (1033). The pubs are thinly scattered from Leeds and Wallasey to Bristol and south Wales, with concentrations in Birmingham, the Black Country and south Warwickshire.

Devenish (Redruth and Weymouth) has responded encouragingly to demands for quality traditional beers, increasing the strength of both its draught beers, and distinguishing between pubs selling real beer and those selling processed substitutes in the list of tied houses it issues. Sadly, however, the list shows that only a small proportion of the 390 Devenish pubs sell real draught beer. The company is under the Whitbread umbrella, too, so that drinkers have further cause for concern. The parent Weymouth brewery produces Wessex best bitter (1042), a dark and full-bodied beer, and an ordinary bitter (1032), whereas Redruth brews Cornish best bitter (1042), a thin ordinary bitter (1033) and XXX (1033), a good dark mild.

Donnington Brewery (Stow-on-the-Wold, Gloucestershire) is owned privately by L. C. Arkell, grandson of Richard Arkell of the Swindon brewing family, who founded the brewery as a private venture in 1865. Picturesquely situated in the valley of the Dikler, north-west of Stow, the brewery stands by a mill pond, and water wheels still provide some of the power for the brewery. Malting was discontinued around 1960, but local ingredients are still used. There are seventeen tied houses, almost all in delightful Cotswold villages, and all of them now offer real draught beer (hand-pumps having recently been installed in the ten pubs that had been converted to pressurized beer). The beers are quite outstanding: XXX dark mild (1033), the delicate and well-hopped light bitter, BB (1033), and the much more robust, malty SBA (1040). Outstanding pubs in which to try them include the Plough at Ford, on the B4077 between Stow and Tewkesbury, and the Snowshill Arms, on the edge of the Cotswold scarp south of Broadway. There are also some free trade outlets around Stratford-upon-Avon and in the Malverns.

Eldridge Pope (Dorchester) dates from 1837, when wine merchant Charles Eldridge bought the Green Dragon Brewery in Dorchester. Business expanded to such an extent that a new brewery was built in 1879; this was burnt down in 1922 and replaced by the present brewery. Two thirds of the 180 tied houses serve pressurized beers only, yet the range and quality of the real beers is remarkable: from the light, sharp Dorchester bitter (1031) through the malty IPA (1041) to the outstanding, recently introduced Royal Oak (1048). The beers, especially Royal Oak, are also widely available in the free trade, from London to Devon, and as far north as Cheltenham. Also brewed is the naturally-conditioned bottled beer, Thomas Hardy Ale (1120), the strongest beer produced in Britain, now brewed annually. Bottles need to be kept for at least four years to mature, and the ale may continue improving in bottle for twenty-five years or more.

Elgood's (Wisbech) has 58 tied houses within thirty miles of the brewery, of which about half sell real draught beer. The North Brink brewery dates from the late eighteenth century, although the present firm was not established until 1905. The brewery has had to deflect a number of unwelcome takeover bids in order to maintain its independence. The beers are a pleasant dark mild (1030) and an unusual, slightly sweet bitter (1037). Amongst the characteristic Fenland pubs owned by Elgood's are the Black Hart at Ring's End, on the A141, and the Rising Sun in Leverington, north-west of Wisbech.

Everard's (Leicester) is in the curious position of having its brewery, in Burton-on-Trent, completely outside its trading area; the Tiger Brewery in Southgate Street, Leicester, was closed in 1931, and has served since then as the distribution centre for the beers. All Everard's beers were converted to chilled and filtered form only in the 1960s, but in 1975 the company began to market Old Original (1050), a strong real draught bitter with a passing resemblance to Ruddle's County. Only a few pubs took Old Original, however, and even some of these dispensed the beer in pressurized form. More recently, though, Everard's Beacon bitter (1037), the full-flavoured Tiger bitter (1041), and the pleasant dark mild (1033) have been made available in real draught form, initially in just one pub, the Globe in Silver Street, Leicester, but now at a rapidly increasing number of outlets. But many of Everard's 160 pubs still sell pressurized beer only.

Felinfoel Brewery (Felinfoel, Llanelli) dates from 1878, when a small brewery was built to supply pubs in and around

Llanelli, and it has grown from these beginnings to its present status as a company controlling 80 tied houses in and around Dyfed and West Glamorgan, with a more far-reaching free trade which includes London. Regrettably, since the beers are highly recommended, most of the outlets use top pressure, although the Sun in Lamb's Conduit Street, London, WC1, for example, offers proof that Double Dragon bitter can travel and still be served traditionally. Apart from Double Dragon (1040), which is a very palatable and distinctive straw-coloured bitter, there is a weaker but still full-flavoured bitter (1035) and a dark mild (1032).

Fuller, Smith & Turner (Chiswick) is one of the few remaining independent London brewers. Brewing has been carried out at the Griffin brewery for over three centuries, although the first Fuller did not take control until the early nineteenth century. There are 110 Fuller's pubs, most of them within twenty miles of the brewery, most of them, too, serving pressurized beer, although the number with real draught beer has increased significantly in the last few years. There is also a widespread free trade, with the emphasis here very much on real beer. The three real beers are all excellent in their own way, and are Extra Special Bitter (1056), a strong, sweet, full-bodied brew which is the strongest bitter in Britain, London Pride (1041), a very palatable ordinary bitter, and Hock (1031), a good, malty dark mild with a pleasant aroma.

Gale's (Horndean, Hampshire) is well known for its superb range of traditional draught beers. The brewery is in the village of Horndean, a few miles north of Portsmouth, and it serves 102 tied houses, all but three of them serving real draught beer. The growth of the company has been modest, with small breweries taken over in Midhurst and Havant, and individual pubs gradually added to the tied estate. This policy of piecemeal acquisition may explain the rather haphazard location of the pubs, which are thick on the ground in east Hampshire and the far west of Sussex, but which can also be found, somewhat unexpectedly, in distant locations – north of Reading, for example, where there are four clustered on or close to the A4074. The beers are XXX mild (1030), a thin light mild; dark mild (1031), which is in relatively few of the pubs; BBB (1037), one of the finest standard bitters in the country; HSB (1051), a powerful and sweet bitter; and, in the winter months only, XXXXX old ale (1045), an excellent sweet and dark beer. Gale's also brews Prize Old Ale (1095), one of the few naturally-conditioned bottled beers, a superb mellow strong ale which improves in bottle up to and beyond ten years.

Gibbs Mew (Salisbury) leapt on to the keg beer bandwagon with some alacrity in the 1960s, brewing three different keg bitters and abandoning cask beer altogether – though by virtue of a fortunate trading agreement draught Bass (confusingly sold in this area as Worthington E) was and is available in some of Gibbs's 55 tied houses. A complete reversal of policy saw the introduction in 1976 of Bishop's Tipple (1067), a sweet barley wine, into some pubs in real draught form, and in the following year premium bitter (1040), a bland ordinary bitter, and Jubilee bitter (1049), rather fuller-flavoured, were introduced. Gibbs was therefore one of a handful of breweries to celebrate the Silver Jubilee with a real draught beer – a product which two years earlier they were not even brewing.

Godson's (Clapton, East London) has recently made the transition from beer wholesalers to brewers, starting in a disused sweet factory in Clapton. Anchor bitter (1043) is a very pale but well-balanced brew made from malt and hops with no added sugar, and was soon on sale in a number of

East London free houses and at the Nag's Head in Hampstead. The capacity of the brewery, London's first new brewery this century, is around fifty barrels a week.

Greenall Whitley (Warrington, Cheshire, and Wem, Shropshire) are the largest of the independent brewers, with about 1,700 pubs supplied from the two breweries. A number of firms has been taken over in Greenall's rise to prominence, and the breweries of most of them have been closed in the relatively recent past: Magee Marshall of Bolton, Groves & Whitnall of Salford, the Chester Northgate Brewery, and the Wrekin Brewery at Wellington in Shropshire. In 1975 the St Helens brewery was closed, to leave Wilderspool brewery in Warrington, where brewing began in 1787, to supply 1,450 pubs in North Wales, north-west England, and southern Scotland. Most of these pubs serve real draught beer, though newer and larger pubs tend to have tank beer. The real beers are a good, consistent bitter (1037) and dark mild (1033), light mild having been suddenly withdrawn in 1977, ostensibly because of falling demand, though reluctance to supply might have been partly to blame. The Wem brewery is still 'independently' run by the Shrewsbury & Wem Brewery Company, although it has been a wholly-owned subsidiary of Greenall Whitley since 1951. The advantages of this delegation of control are clear – an impressive profit performance, soaring output (it has increased fourfold in ten years) and excellent real draught beer in all the 225 pubs. There are three varieties – a superb, dry mild (1032), a light and refreshing pale ale (1031) and a well-hopped bitter (1038). Shipstone's was bought in 1978.

Greene King (Biggleswade and Bury St Edmunds) is, like Greenall Whitley, one of the half-dozen independent brewery companies with a regional rather than local influence. (It also owns Rayment's brewery at Furneaux Pelham in

Hertfordshire, but that company still trades separately, and is dealt with in its own right in this chapter). The two breweries supply four different draught beers to around 850 pubs in East Anglia, but there is a preference for top-pressure dispense and real beer is in only about a quarter of the pubs – often the smaller, more remote country pubs at that. This is a real tragedy, since draught Abbot ale (1048), a magnificent, strong and yet quite bitter brew, is one of the most distinctive and highly regarded draught bitters in the country. The other beers are IPA (1035), a reasonable bitter; dark mild (1031); and, at Biggleswade only, KK light mild (1031), thin but palatable.

Greenwood's (Greenwich) is a venture which grew out of Alan Greenwood's chain of real ale off-licences in London suburbs. The 'brewery' is located in the former Lovibond's plant in Greenwich. The old brewery, which was closed down in 1960, has been renamed the Straightsmouth Brewery, and production was to start in 1978. The re-opening was delayed by a number of setbacks, and Greenwood's beer is now available in a number of London free houses, but is brewed at the West Crown brewery in Newark, Nottinghamshire. It now looks unlikely that the Lovibond's plant will be brought back into production.

Guernsey Brewery (St Peter Port, Guernsey) is the larger of the two independent breweries on the island, with about 50 tied houses and a considerable free trade. Two draught beers are brewed: a pleasant bitter (1045), available only at the Golden Lion in St Peter Port in draught form – until 1977 it had been pressure-dispensed in all outlets since the 1960s – and a strong but rather bland dark mild, LBA (1037), which is served direct from the cask or on handpump in about a dozen bars.

Hall & Woodhouse (Blandford Forum, Dorset) dates from 1777, when the Ansty brewery was founded by Charles Hall in the village of Ansty, to the west of Blandford. In 1882 the brewery was moved to its present site beside the River Stour at Blandford St Mary. There are now around 170 tied houses selling Badger beers, about half of which offer traditional draught beers – one or both of PA (1031), a thin but pleasant beer which is also known as boy's bitter, and best bitter (1041), a superb dry but richly flavoured bitter. Best bitter is also increasingly available in the free trade. During the past few years the apparently inevitable progress towards top-pressure dispense in Hall & Woodhouse pubs has been reversed, and many pubs have been supplied with handpumps; one such pub (though it was previously selling real beer, direct from the cask) is the Ship, at the corner of Tout Hill and Bleke Street in Shaftesbury, Dorset, a superb seventeenth-century local which has both Badger beers.

Hanson's: See Banks's

Hardy's & Hanson's (Kimberley, Nottinghamshire) is the result of the merger in 1930 of two breweries which had been in competition literally across the street from each other for almost a century. Robinson's brewery, founded in 1832, was taken over by William and Thomas Hardy in 1857, while across the road Hanson's had begun brewing in 1847. Some tank beer is produced, and some outlets use pressure-dispense, but most of the 200 pubs selling Kimberley Ales have real draught beer. The two beers are a refreshing, well-hopped bitter (1039) and a strong and satisfying dark mild (1035). Kimberley pubs are commonest to the west of Nottingham, although there are also some in Derbyshire, Leicestershire and Lincolnshire.

Hartley's (Ulverston, Cumbria) is an outstanding example of a small independent brewery providing an excellent choice of very good real draught beers. By virtue of a trading agreement it also supplies real draught beer to some Whitbread houses, as well as to all 57 of its own pubs. The pubs, mostly in and around the southern Lake District, serve one or more of dark mild (1032), a delicately flavoured bitter (1032) and the magnificent, quite sweet, full-drinking strong bitter, XB (1041). There is also a flourishing free trade.

Harvey's (Lewes, East Sussex) was founded in 1790 by John Harvey, and the Bridge Wharf brewery still stands on the original site by the River Ouse in the centre of Lewes. The cellars and the fermenting block are original, but the rest of the brewery, including the brewhouse with its attractive tower, dates from 1880. The capacity of the brewery is about 500 barrels a week, supplying a substantial free trade in Sussex and Kent, together with 50 tied pubs (half of which belong to Beard's, a separate company, also in Lewes, but one which no longer brews, and gets all its beer from Harvey's). About half the pubs have real beer, of which there is an impressive range: XX mild (1030), two bitters named PA (1033) and BB (1040), the dark and fruity XXXX winter brew (1041) and Elizabethan barley wine (1090), a pale and exceptionally strong brew which is only occasionally sold on draught.

Henley Brewery: see Brakspear's.

Higson's (Liverpool) beers are now essentially available only in and around Merseyside, following the sale of their seven pubs in the Potteries to Banks's. The brewery in Stanhope Street was founded in 1780, and there are now 157 pubs, half of which sell real ale. Draught Bass is available in a number of pubs under a trading agreement – Bass Charrington have a substantial shareholding – but Higson's own beers are a pleasant dark mild (1033) and a popular bitter (1038).

Holden's (Woodsetton, West Midlands) are the largest of the three small Black Country brewers. Their ten pubs are supplemented by a surprisingly extensive free trade, from Stafford to Bristol (although the outlets are thinly scattered) and by a considerable bottling operation. Most of the tied houses serve real draught beer, although in most cases only the mild is available (a reminder of the campaign to promote Holden's keg bitter: 'Holden's Golden, the beer with the glow'). The Park Inn, next to the brewery, and the Old Mill in Upper Gornal are among those with the full range of beers, which are a highly regarded dark mild (1035), an excellent though fairly sweet bitter (1039), a stronger special bitter (1052) which is too sweet for many tastes, and an outstanding dark old ale (1075) which is available for a very short season around Christmas and the New Year.

Holt's (Manchester) is one of the most uncompromisingly traditional and fiercely independent of the surviving local brewers, and its policy of providing cheap real beer of excellent quality has been rewarded with a remarkable profits record over the past few years. There are 80 pubs, largely in the north Manchester and Salford areas, all using handpumps or electric pumps to dispense a good dark mild (1033) and a superb and much sought-after bitter (1038), of which the local CAMRA guide says that 'the biting flavour is uncompromisingly acerbic, but the taste, once acquired, can become pleasantly addictive.'

Home Brewery (Nottingham) dates from 1890, when the company was formed to acquire Robinson's brewery in Daybrook, on the outskirts of the city. Steady expansion has seen the number of tied houses reach 400, of which a substantial majority serve real draught beer – an excellent and good-value bitter (1038) and an acceptable dark mild (1036). Home Brewery pubs can be found in most of the East Midlands, and as far afield as south Yorkshire, Northampton and the Lincolnshire coast.

Hook Norton Brewery (Hook Norton, near Banbury) is the smallest of the four surviving commercial breweries in Oxfordshire. The business was started by John Harris in a farmhouse in the village in 1849, and the present imposing tower brewery dates from 1899. The first Clarke to enter the business – Bill Clarke and his grandson run the brewery now – appeared in 1887. Nowadays there are 34 pubs, all offering traditional draught beer, namely Hookey light mild (1032), best bitter (1036) and, in a few pubs, the relatively recently introduced Old Hookey (1049), which is a dark winter brew with a traditional old ale taste.

Hoskins (Leicester) is a curious company which has a small brewery in Beaumanor Road, Leicester, two off-licences in the city, and only one tied house, the Red Lion, some fifteen miles west at Market Bosworth. Free trade is surprisingly small, too, since the beers are normally of very high quality. The original brewhouse, built in 1895, is still in use, and the business has been run by the Hoskins family since Tom Hoskins took over in 1911. The untimely death of George Hoskins recently led to fears that capital transfer tax might mean the end of the brewery, yet the firm has carried on, producing dark mild (1033), a slightly variable but distinctive bitter (1038) and – for sale in casks only, to order – old ale (1039), a dark beer which is the bitter with added caramel and priming sugar.

Hull Brewery (Kingston-upon-Hull), renamed North Country Breweries since having been taken over by Northern

Foods in 1972, has rough-filtered all its beer since the 1920s, and though it has recently renamed its beers 'Old Tradition', thereby leaping on to the real ale bandwagon, it has persisted in policies of installing cellar tanks and pressure-dispense, and in removing traditional handpumps. The beers are a thin dark mild (1032) and a bitter (1037).

Hyde's (Manchester) has been brewing at the Anvil brewery in Moss Lane West since the end of the nineteenth century, though the brewery was known as the Queen's Brewery until 1944. There are about 50 tied houses, mostly in south Manchester, though there are two in the city centre, and half a dozen as far afield as Wrexham. All of them offer at least one real beer, usually from electric pumps; all four draught beers are dry hopped, and they comprise dark mild (1032), a dry, popular and light best mild (1034), a standard bitter (1036), and Anvil strong ale (1068), a dark winter brew reintroduced in 1975. Bitter and dark mild sell roughly equal amounts, light mild half as much, so that Hyde's is one of the few brewers to sell more mild than bitter.

Jennings (Cockermouth, Cumbria) brews in possibly the most spectacular surroundings of any brewery in Britain – in a stone-built brewhouse on the banks of the River Cocker at the foot of Cockermouth Castle. Its successful fight for independence has already been noted in Chapter 4; to the great relief of the northern Lake District, its real draught beers are still available: a magnificent, really sharp bitter (1035) and a very good dark mild (1033). All but two of the 90 Jennings pubs sell real ale.

Kimberley: see Hardy's & Hanson's.

King & Barnes (Horsham, West Sussex) results from the amalgamation in 1906 of the businesses founded by James

King, who was brewing at The Bishopric, the present site, by 1870, and the Barnes at the East Street Brewery in Horsham. Today the beers are produced from East Anglian barley, a small amount of flaked maize, Kent and Worcester hops, invert sugar, yeast and water. All three draught beers are dry hopped. Only three of the 58 tied pubs use top pressure: the rest serve one or more of XX mild (1032), which is dark and sweet, PA bitter (1035), a dry and heavily-hopped beer, and – in the winter months only – XXXX old ale (1047), a rather sweet but full-flavoured strong dark ale, by traditional means.

Lees (Middleton, Greater Manchester) was founded in 1828 on its present site in Middleton Junction; the present brewery was erected nearly fifty years later. John Willie Lees, as it is locally known, now has some 200 tied houses, virtually all of them using traditional means of dispense, although both the free and tied trade in north Wales tend towards bright beer because of the seasonal nature of demand. A fine range of beers is offered in Manchester, Lancashire and Cheshire: a light mild (1031), a pleasant dark and full-bodied best mild (1035), bitter (1038) and – a newish introduction – Moonraker strong ale (1074), sweet, rich, and dark.

Lion Ales: see Brown.

Litchborough Brewery (Litchborough, Northamptonshire) has already been discussed in Chapter 4, where its establishment by ex-Watney brewer Bill Urquhart was traced. Regrettably, all the beer was filtered until recently, though casks of Northamptonshire bitter (1038) can now be bought in fined form; top pressure, however, is used in most of the free trade outlets.

Lorimer's: see Vaux.

Maclay's (Alloa) is one of the two surviving independent commercial breweries in Scotland, although Bass Charrington's thirty per cent shareholding poses a distinct question mark over their continuing independence. The twenty-five tied houses use top pressure or air pressure to serve the beers – 60/– light (1030), 70/– SPA (1035) and the darkish, pleasant 80/– export bitter (1040). Unpressurized Maclay's can be very good indeed, but it is hard to find.

Marston's (Burton-on-Trent)–properly Marston, Thompson & Evershed – is one of the four remaining breweries in Burton-on-Trent. The present business was formed by the mergers of Marston's Horninglow Brewery with Thompson & Sons in 1898, and with Sidney Evershed Ltd in 1905. The company has never been afraid to enter the takeover market, and through acquisitions in Winchester, Worcester, Manchester, Penrith and elsewhere has become a regional brewery with over 600 tied houses spread throughout England. Whitbread's large stake in Marston's may lead to the final merger for the company, however. There is an outstanding range of draught beers, served naturally in the majority of the pubs: a well-flavoured, creamy dark mild (1032), the remarkable and distinctive Merrie Monk mild (1043: the strongest mild in the country), Burton bitter (1037), the superb, fairly strong, malty Pedigree bitter (1043), and Owd Roger (1080), a sweet and heavy barley wine first brewed at the Royal Standard of England at Forty Green in Buckinghamshire.

McMullen's (Hertford), sole survivor of the thirty-five Hertfordshire brewing companies which entered the twentieth century, was founded in 1827 by Peter McMullen, great-grandfather of the present chairman. Very much a family-run business, McMullen's has 162 pubs in and around Hertfordshire, but only about a quarter serve real draught beer, and sadly the company prefers to see blanket pressure used. The beers are AK light mild (1033) and the unusual, fruity yet well-hopped Country bitter (1041).

Mitchell's (Lancaster) is one of two small brewers in the city of Lancaster. William Mitchell began to brew at the Black Horse in Common Garden Street in 1861, transferred to the New Inn in 1874, and behind it built the brewery which is still in use today. Nowadays the Barkers, descendants of the founder, run the company, and after a flirtation with keg in the 1960s they appear to have chosen to promote their real draught beers, in particular the sweet, full-flavoured extra special bitter (1044), but also a malty ordinary bitter (1037) and a pleasant dark mild (1032) which is nowadays less commonly available. There are 47 tied houses, of which only three fail to give the drinker the opportunity of tasting Mitchell's beers in real draught form.

Morland's (Abingdon, Oxfordshire) brews some of the most distinctive and highly praised real draught beer in the country, yet it serves it without top pressure in only a minority of its 220 pubs. A very real threat on the horizon is posed by Whitbread, which has increased its shareholding to 39 per cent and which has consistently been rumoured to be planning a bid. The beers are the magnificent, fairly dark XX mild (1032), a good bitter (1035) and BB (1042), a superb, full-bodied yet sharp strong bitter. Notable pubs include the Cricketers' Arms in Iffley Road, Oxford, and the Shepherd's Hut at Ewelme, Oxfordshire.

Morrell's (Oxford), like its Abingdon neighbours, has relied heavily upon top-pressure dispense in the past, but there are welcome signs that real beer is becoming more widely available. The brewery, still in the hands of the Morrell family, controls 140 pubs within a radius of thirty miles. No less than six draught beers are produced, all but the strongest of them being brewed in conical fermenters, and both flaked maize and glucose are added to the barley malt. The beers are a refreshing light ale (1031), dark mild (1032), a rather bland bitter (1036), the strong and fuller-flavoured Varsity bitter (1041), and two very strong beers, both of which are fairly rare in draught form – College Ale (1073), a rich, dark winter brew, and Celebration Ale (1066), a sweet, heavy pale beer which is occasionally to be found on draught. Dark mild and Varsity bitter are only in a restricted number of outlets, but the Black Boy in the Oxford suburb of Headington sells the whole range of Morrell's beers.

North Country Breweries: see Hull.

Okell's (Douglas, Isle of Man) has about seventy tied houses on the island, all of them serving real draught beer made at the Falcon Brewery, which was founded by William Okell in Castle Hill, Douglas, in the middle of the nineteenth century, the present buildings dating from 1875. The two draught beers are an excellent draught mild (1035) which is in most but not all of the pubs, and a well-hopped best bitter (1036); both brews, of course, have to conform to the island's Pure Beer Act.

Oldham Brewery (Oldham, Greater Manchester) produces a traditional mild and bitter at the Coldhurst Street brewery, but the trend in new and modernized houses seems to be towards bright beer in equally characterless surroundings, and if this trend continues only Oldham's traditional pubs will serve real draught dark mild (1031) and bitter (1037) – the latter a much sought-after pale, full-bodied drink. Currently less than a quarter of the 100 tied houses have real ale.

An apparent takeover bid from Northern Foods (keen to link their Hull brewery with others in the north) was thwarted in 1975, but members of the Big Six are thought to have an interest in the firm, and so real beer drinkers may be in for a thin time.

Paine's (St Neots) is one of the smallest surviving breweries in the country, with just twenty-four tied houses, although the firm operates mainly as a maltster. All the pubs were converted to pressure-dispense in the 1960s, but the demand for real beer was recognized and three were switched back to traditional dispense early in 1975. Later in the same year a new strong bitter, EG or Eynesbury Giant (1048), was launched to complement the light, rather sweet XXX bitter (1037) and extra special mild (1032). One or more of these beers is now served in real draught form in fourteen of the tied houses. A light mild (1031) was introduced in 1978.

Palmer's (Bridport, Dorset) produces two real bitters in a thatched brewery dating from 1794, complete with the oldest working water-wheel in south-west England. The chairman has said of the brewery that 'we've tried to preserve its traditional image' though this is hardly true of the beers, which are mostly served by top pressure, or of the policy of discarding low-turnover pubs – twenty-five or so have been off-loaded, leaving around seventy tied houses. The beers, when served traditionally, by handpump or direct from the cask, can be excellent, especially IPA (1039); there is also the thin and rather bland BB (1030).

Penrhos Court (Kington, Herefordshire) has been discussed in detail in Chapter 4, so that all that is necessary here is to list the beers – the malty, full-bodied Penrhos bitter (1042) and the distinctive Jones's Ale (1050), together with two less common brews, the very potent special bitter (1060) and porter (1045), which is an attempt to re-create the bitter stout popular in the eighteenth century.

Pollard's (Stockport), another of Britain's newer brewers, has also been examined in the previous chapter. The beer in this case is John Barleycorn bitter (1036), sold in a number of freehouses thinly spread around the country, including the White Gates, CAMRA Investments' pub in Hyde, and the Midway in Stockport. Indeed, John Barleycorn bitter has even been sold in Cornwall.

Randall's (St Peter Port, Guernsey) brews two draught beers at its Vauxlaurens brewery, which has been in operation for three hundred years. They have seventeen tied houses, although most of the trade on Guernsey is free from tie, and is shared with the Guernsey Brewery, and with suppliers of keg beer from the mainland and from Jersey. Bobby mild (1035) is a thin, unusual dark mild sold in the public bars of about ten pubs and hotels, although the number selling it seems to be declining. Best bitter (1044), an extremely palatable pale but strong brew, was for some time available in real draught form only at the Royal Arms in St Peter Port, but is now also in the Sporting Club, St Peter Port, and the Imperial Hotel at La Lague, Pleinmont.

Rayment's (Furneaux Pelham, Hertfordshire) was established in 1860, but was purchased in 1888 by Frederick King and one of his fellow Greene King directors. Initially Rayment's was operated as a separate private partnership, but it became a subsidiary of Greene King in 1928, although somewhat surprisingly it has maintained a separate identity, with its own range of beers. Indeed, there has been substantial expansion recently, with Rayment's bitter increasingly popular in the free trade, which now takes 90 per cent of production, and the number of brews a week has been stepped up from three to five, totalling 300 barrels a week. AK mild (1031), a pale mild which is hard to find on draught and in fact is mostly bottled, and BBA (1036), a tasty and highly regarded bitter, are the two brews, served by traditional methods in only nine of Rayment's twenty-five tied houses. Real draught bitter is much more widely available in the free trade.

Ridley's (Chelmsford, Essex) has its offices in Chelmsford, but the brewery is in the near-by village of Hartford End, where the business was founded in the 1840s. Two really outstanding draught beers are brewed: a creamy, slightly sweet dark mild (1030) and a subtle, refreshing bitter (1034). The beers are supplied in traditional form to all but one of the 65 tied houses, although the mild is in by no means all of them; indeed, it accounts for only a tiny fraction of output, and there must be fears for its survival. The tied estate is highly concentrated in the immediate vicinity of the brewery, but there is also quite a bit of free trade, as far away as London.

Ringwood Brewery (Ringwood, Hampshire) is run by Peter Austin, formerly the head brewer at Hull Brewery and more recently involved in setting up the Penrhos Court brewery. The brewery at Ringwood is a modern stainless-steel plant with a capacity of around sixty barrels a week. Production began in April 1978, and the plan at that time was to brew two different real draught beers from an all-malt recipe with no adjuncts or additives. Free houses in Hampshire and Dorset showed considerable interest in stocking the beer, the first to be brewed in Ringwood since 1923. The beers are bitter (1040) and Fortyniner (1049).

Robinson's (Stockport, Greater Manchester) dates from the 1860s and has grown by taking over a number of other breweries, notably Kay's Atlas Brewery in Manchester and Bell's of Stockport. There are now about 320 tied pubs, only one of them using carbon-dioxide pressure, and they can be found in Greater Manchester, Lancashire, Cheshire, the Peak District and North Wales. The beers produced are best mild (1032), a pale mild which is Robbies' biggest seller; dark mild (1032), the best mild with caramel added, which is sent to only one or two pubs, such as the Old Pack Horse in Chapel-en-le-Frith; bitter (1035), which is also not in many pubs; and best bitter (1042), a potent and well-balanced brew which is far more popular. On draught in the winter months only is Old Tom (1079), a quite magnificent strong ale.

Ruddle's (Langham, Rutland), one of the leaders of the real-ale revolution, first took over the brewery at Langham in 1911, although it had been established in the middle of the nineteenth century. There has been considerable development recently, with two major expansions within two years in the mid-1970s. There is only one tied house (35 were sold in 1978, most of them to Everard's and Sam Smith's), but the free trade – somcthing like 200 outlets in southern England, East Anglia and the Midlands – overwhelmingly takes real draught beer, predominantly Ruddle's County (1050), one of the cult beers of the 1970s, but nevertheless an excellent, dark, malty, strong bitter, though there is also a bitter (1032), which is light but eminently drinkable. Rutland barley wine (1080) has intermittently been sold on draught.

St Austell Brewery (St Austell, Cornwall) was established in 1851 and the present managing director is the great-grandson of the founder, Walter Hicks. Expansion over the years has seen the acquisition of breweries in Wadebridge, Hayle and Penryn, and there are now 132 St Austell pubs, more than half of them selling real draught beer – XXXX dark mild (1032), the light and unusual bitter, BB (1031), which can be an acquired taste, and the newly introduced strong bitter named after the founder, Hicks Special (1050).

Selby Brewery (Selby, North Yorkshire) was reopened in 1972 after a gap in brewing of eighteen years, as explained in Chapter 4. There is a certain amount of free trade, but only one tied house, the Board Inn at Howden on north Humberside. Production, though, is little more than three barrels a week. The beers brewed have in some cases been experimental – Nut Brown Ale, for example, a mild brewed at an original gravity of 1035 to a pre-war recipe, was withdrawn after a couple of months' trial in 1976 – but they seem to be settled now as special pale ale (1036), a bitter which, probably because of the limited size of the brewery, is somewhat variable, and strong ale (1048), a fairly dark and potent beer. Brahms & Liszt special pale ale (1048) is a bottle-conditioned brew produced especially for the Leeds pub of that name. Three other bottle-conditioned beers.

Shepherd Neame (Faversham) is now the only independent brewery in Kent, and in an area where choice is limited and pressurized beer all too common, has greatly benefited by supplying distinctive real draught beers. Reporting a 40 per cent free-trade sales increase in 1975, chairman Robert Neame stressed 'the demand of the public for something different from national beers served under pressure'. There are 234 tied houses, all but a handful of which serve draught beer which is characteristically well-hopped, clean-tasting and really bitter. The dark mild (1031) is unspectacular, but the bitter (1036) and the slightly sweeter best bitter (1039) are both extremely good, and the stock ale (1039), an old ale with an unusual combination of tastes, is well worth a try. Stock ale and best bitter are in relatively few of the pubs, but all four beers can be sampled in the unspoilt Walnut Tree at Dean Street, south of Maidstone.

Shipstone's (Nottingham) Star brewery was established in 1852 in the suburb of New Basford by James Shipstone, and the ornate Victorian buildings are still very much in use today, producing fine traditional ales for 250 pubs, almost all of which serve the beer naturally. The celebrated and distinctive beers are a well-hopped and dryish-tasting dark mild (1035) and a superb light-coloured bitter (1038) which is dry hopped. The most convenient pub in Nottingham for rail travellers, and one which sells excellent Shippo's, is the Queen's Hotel opposite the station. Northern Foods made a takeover bid for the company in 1978; thankfully the shareholders opted for independence and local control, and indeed a mere 4 per cent of the shares were committed to Northern before the dairy firm allowed the bid to lapse. But Greenall's bought Shipstone's later in 1978.

Simpkiss (Brierley Hill, West Midlands), one of the small Black Country breweries, was formed by the merger of Johnson & Phipps of Wolverhampton with J. P. Simpkiss in 1955. There are now sixteen tied houses served from the Dennis Brewery in Brettell Lane, fifteen of them selling real ale, though the mild is pressurized in an increasing number of them. The nationwide plight of mild is summed up by the fortunes of one small brewery in a traditional mild stronghold: 'A pint of mild is the lifeblood of the Black Country. We used to sell two pints of mild for every one of bitter, but now it's the other way round.' Simpkiss dark mild (1034) is, however, generally recognized as unspectacular, although its sweet, pale and delicately flavoured bitter (1039) is a superb drink. An unusual old ale (1050) is also available in the winter months.

Smiles Brewery (Bristol) now operates from a brewhouse in Colston Yard in the centre of Bristol, although Smiles bitter (1037) was first brewed by John Payne solely for his restaurant, Bell's Diner in York Road, in 1977. The Colston Yard brewhouse is capable of producing up to thirty barrels a week, and the beer is available in several free houses in and around Bristol.

Samuel Smith (Tadcaster, North Yorkshire) brews at the oldest brewery in Yorkshire, and still uses slate Yorkshire squares in the fermenting room. The strain of yeast used has been unchanged since the turn of the century, and wooden casks are used for all its real beer, so that the image of traditionalism is prevalent. There are more than 300 tied houses, mostly selling real beer, namely Old Brewery Bitter (1040), a malty and full-flavoured brew. 4X light mild was withdrawn in cask-conditioned form in 1976. There is a very extensive free trade covering much of England and Wales.

South Wales Clubs (Pontyclun, Mid-Glamorgan) is the only one of the two surviving clubs breweries to produce real beer, which is sent to about one-third of the 350 clubs supplied, and to a few free-trade pubs, especially in the Bristol area. Two different bitters are produced at the Crown Brewery: CPA (1033) and the heavier, pleasant SBB (1036).

Timothy Taylor (Keighley, West Yorkshire). Founded in Cook Lane, Keighley, in 1858 by Timothy Taylor, the firm moved to larger premises at the present site in Knowle Spring in 1863, and is now a small private company with twenty-eight tied houses. The business is still family-controlled, and no less than six draught beers are brewed, one or more being served in real draught form in every tied house. The beers are dark mild (1033); golden best (1033), which is a light mild; bitter (1033), fairly similar to golden best; best bitter (1037), a distinctive bitter held in very high regard locally; Landlord (1042), a very popular and palatable strong bitter; and Ram Tam (1043), a full-bodied dark winter brew.

Theakston's (Masham, North Yorkshire, and Carlisle) has had a chequered history in recent years, as was suggested in Chapter 4. The firm's free trade has expanded enormously and now covers an area from Scotland to Kent and Devon, but the tied houses have been progressively sold off and now number only four. Nowadays the best bitter (1038) is brewed at Carlisle – which may explain the thinner, less distinctive flavour many Theakston's drinkers have noticed – whereas light mild (1032), the similar dark mild (1032), and the renowned Old Peculier (1060) are still brewed at Masham.

Thwaites (Blackburn), whose tied estate grew dramatically with post-war acquisitions of breweries in Bury and Preston, began a major reconstruction of its Star Brewery in 1964, yet even at this stage of the keg boom its commitment to traditional draught beer never wavered, and today 360 of their 380 tied houses serve real beer. The three beers are a superb, creamy dark mild (1031), a rather lighter best mild (1033) and a very good, light, well-hopped bitter (1036).

Tolly Cobbold (Ipswich) was inevitably going to be taken over: anyone watching the brewery scene in 1976–7 must have reached that conclusion, as profits failed to reflect assets and shares responded to stock market rumours. Northern Foods, owners of Hull Brewery, bought more than a tenth of the shares and was rumoured to be bidding late in 1976; in mid-1977 the theory was that Bass Charrington, also with a ten per cent holding, had made a takeover approach; yet in August 1977 it was Ellerman Lines, the shipping company which controlled Cameron's, which effected the takeover, with the agreement of Tolly's directors. The beers, at least, should remain the same, uninspiring to many, yet rousing fierce loyalty in others: mild (1030), a pleasant bitter (1034), the sweeter Cantab bitter (1041) and the unusual winter brew, Old Strong (1047). Only a third of the 360 tied pubs sell real beer, though there have been encouraging signs recently that the number may increase.

Vaux (Sunderland) also owns Lorimer's (Edinburgh) and Ward's, which trade much more independently and are dealt with separately in this list. Vaux is therefore one of the largest of the independent brewers, but real draught beer is only rarely available in the 500 houses served from Sunderland, where the beers are the almost non-existent (in real draught form) dark mild (1030), the very pleasant, dry Samson strong bitter (1042) and the bland, newly introduced Sunderland draught bitter (1040). Lorimer's cask-conditioned bitter (1036) is available in a small minority of the pubs served from the Edinburgh brewery, as well as in some Vaux pubs. Darley's were taken over in 1978.

Wadworth's (Devizes, Wiltshire), whose Northgate Brewery dominates the small market town of Devizes, also dominates the town and the surrounding area with its pubs, many of which are delightful country pubs, and almost all of which serve real draught beer. The brewery was built in 1885, and the company has as its present chairman the great-nephew of the founder. Tradition is highly valued: a cooper's shop is maintained to repair the wooden barrels, shire horses are used for local deliveries, and after a short-lived venture into top-pressure dispense Wadworth's is now committed to real draught beer in the vast majority of their outlets – 143 tied houses together with a considerable free trade in southern and south-west England. Four draught beers are brewed, ranging from PA (1031) through the superb, light, but delicately-flavoured IPA (1035) to the much-vaunted, full-bodied but rather sweet 6X (1039) and Old Timer (1053), a magnificent strong brew which is normally on sale in the winter months only.

Ward's (Sheffield) was taken over by Vaux Breweries in 1972, but retains its own draught beers and its own identity. The only independent brewers in the Sheffield area, it now brews two cask-conditioned beers at the Sheaf Brewery on the Eccleshall Road, having discontinued its ordinary bitter at the end of 1976. The beers are best mild (1034), a dark and malty brew, and Sheffield best bitter (1038), a popular, slightly sweet beer which is full of flavour. The beers are served by traditional methods in the majority of the ninety-five pubs.

Wells (Bedford) was established in Horne Lane, Bedford, in 1876, and the site was used for a hundred years until Wells' brand-new brewery on the edge of Bedford was opened in 1976. Fortunately the company decided to retain the capability to brew traditional draught beers, though the temptation must have been to build a keg factory. It is all the more surprising, then, to find that less than a hundred of the 265 tied houses serve real beer – IPA (1036), an instantly recognizable bitter with many devotees, and Fargo (1051), a dark strong bitter.

West Crown (Newark, Nottinghamshire) began producing real draught beer in the autumn of 1977 – thus reintroducing the craft to a town which John Smith's, the northern arm of Courage, had all but converted to bright beer. Brothers Norman and Alan Rutherford chose an old maltings as the site for their brewery, which is capable of producing 500 barrels a week. The beer, the pleasant, fairly dark Regal bitter (1037), is brewed from an all-malt recipe, and is available in free houses over a wide area of the East Midlands and even further afield, although in Newark itself it is in the Old Kings Arms. Also brews, Greenwood's No. 8 (1037) and No. 10 (1042).

Wolverhampton & Dudley: see Banks's.

Yates & Jackson (Lancaster) first took over the Old Brewery in the nineteenth century, although parts of the brewery buildings date from 1669. The firm is totally traditional, having never produced keg beers, and since the bottling plant broke down in 1974 only draught beers have been produced for the 43 tied houses. Virtually no advertising is undertaken – some of the pubs have no brewer's sign outside – yet the quality of the beer is sufficient to attract drinkers. The beers are a very acceptable and quite sharp dark mild (1030) and an outstanding ordinary bitter (1035), subtly flavoured but with a very bitter palate.

Young's (Wandsworth, London) is one of the best-known producers of traditional draught beer, and all of their 135 pubs, many of which are very close indeed to the brewery, serve real ale. Horse-drawn drays make deliveries to those pubs which lie within three miles of the brewery, and two nineteenth-century beam engines still supply much of the power. The four real beers are best malt ale (1030), which is a rather nondescript mild; a superb, subtle and sharp ordinary bitter (1036); special bitter (1046), which is much sweeter but full-flavoured; and Winter Warmer (1055), a distinctive old ale. The beers are also extensively available in the free trade in the Home Counties and as far away as Oxford.

The National Brewers

Allied Breweries – Ansell's, Ind Coope and Tetley's – have five breweries producing real draught beer, and some of it is excellent, although until recently the tendency has been for it to be retained only in older, smaller, unmodernized houses. Thankfully, newer and refurbished houses are now more likely to have real ale, especially in the south of England, although there are welcome signs further north. *Ind Coope* is responsible for two breweries: at Romford the bitter (1037) seems to have been improved, but there is a lack of real flavour to the KK light mild (1031), whereas at Burton the very pleasant bitter (1037) has been joined by Draught Burton Ale (1047), a superb full-bodied bitter with a dry palate. Launched in mid-1976, the Burton Ale, which is brewed from the same basic recipe as bottled Double Diamond (the keg version is a great deal weaker, sweeter and, of course, gassier), has been an outstanding success in London and south-east England, and is now available in several hundred pubs, always in real draught form.

The Birmingham brewery of *Ansell's* has traditionally been famous for its dark mild (1035), one of the outstanding mild ales of a region famous for them. More recently the rather more mediocre Ansell's bitter (1037) has been vigorously promoted by the late, unlamented Ansell's bittermen. A new bitter (1045) was launched in 1978. Too often Ansell's pubs offer only pressurized bitter alongside the draught mild, and many of the newer pubs have no real beer at all. *Tetley's* run breweries at Leeds, and, as Tetley Walker, at Warrington. Tetley's bitter (1036) is an extremely popular drink in west Yorkshire (where there are in any case few alternatives), and is a good ordinary bitter; the dark mild (1032) is equally acceptable: both are usually drunk through a tight, creamy head. Walker's bitter (1036), a

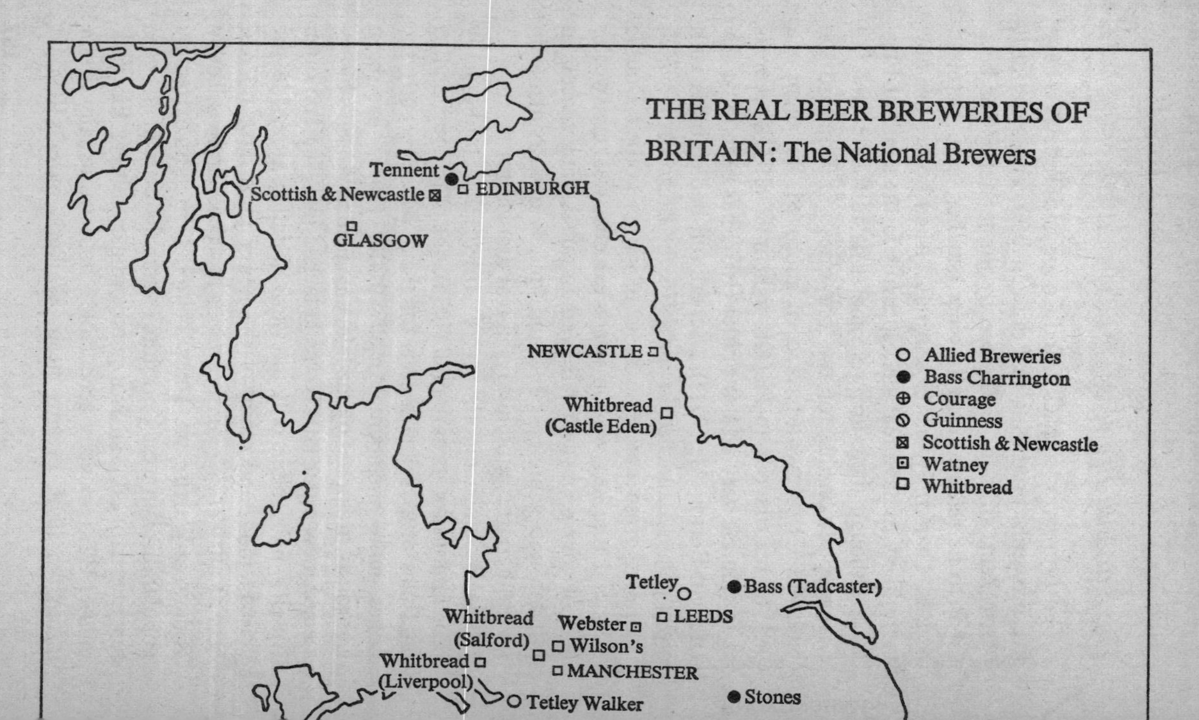
THE REAL BEER BREWERIES OF
BRITAIN: The National Brewers
Allied Breweries
Bass Charrington
Courage
Guinness
Scottish & Newcastle
Watney
Whitbread
Tennent
Scottish & Newcastle
EDINBURGH
GLASGOW
NEWCASTLE
Whitbread
(Castle Eden)
Tetley
Bass (Tadcaster)
LEEDS
Webster
Wilson's
MANCHESTER
Whitbread
(Salford)
Whitbread
(Liverpool)
Tetley Walker
Stones

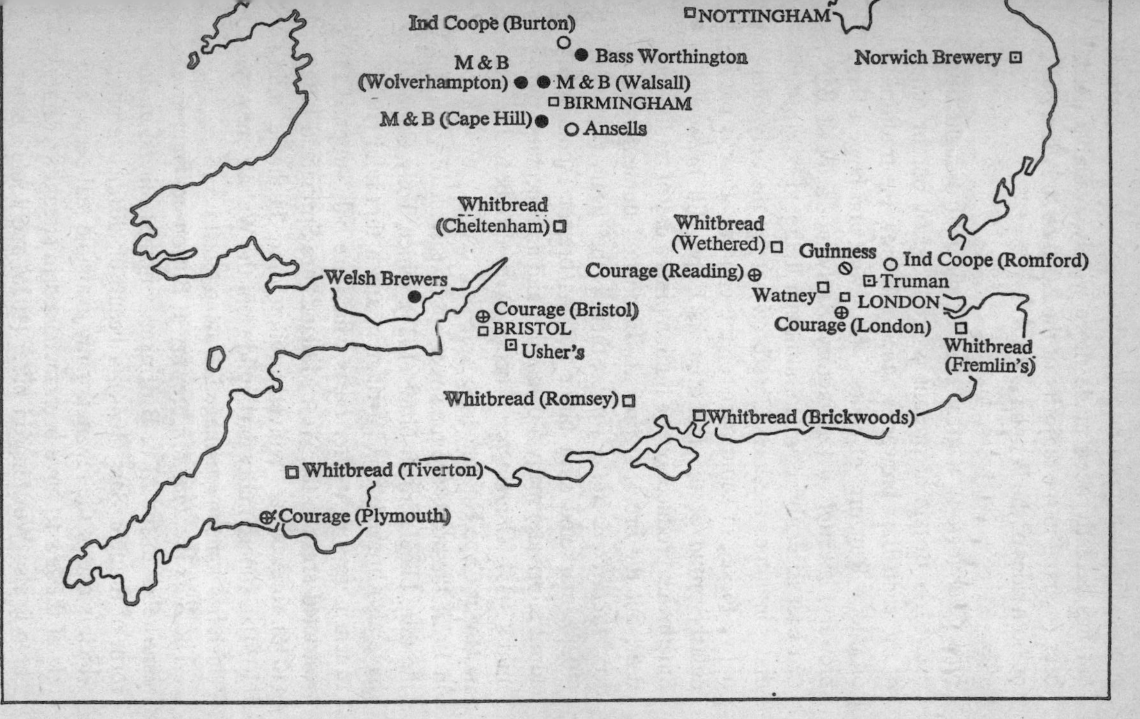

NOTTINGHAM
Ind Coope (Burton)
Bass Worthington
Norwich Brewery
M & B (Wolverhampton)
M & B (Walsall)
BIRMINGHAM
M & B (Cape Hill)
Ansells
Whitbread (Cheltenham)
Whitbread (Wethered)
Guinness
Ind Coope (Romford)
Courage (Reading)
Truman
Welsh Brewers
Watney
LONDON
Courage (Bristol)
BRISTOL
Courage (London)
Usher's
Whitbread (Fremlin's)
Whitbread (Romsey)
Whitbread (Brickwoods)
Whitbread (Tiverton)
Courage (Plymouth)

superb, lightly-hopped bitter, seemed doomed to extinction but has recently been made more widely available. Real beer is served in the majority of the 2,000 or so Allied pubs on both sides of the Pennines.

Bass Charrington: a great deal of the real draught beer brewed in Britain at present is produced by one or other of the eight Bass breweries which still brew the traditional product – Runcorn, of course, the newest and biggest Bass brewery, is simply a keg factory. Sadly, not a lot of Bass real beer is highly regarded, although it should be stressed that sometimes the local Bass brew can be the only alternative to keg in some parts of the country. Bass is particularly proud of the fact that its Cape Hill brewery in Smethwick produces over a million pints a day of traditional beer, but the brews are mostly bland and unmemorable: for *Mitchell's & Butler's* pubs, there is the sugary Brew XI (1038), marketed as a bitter but (as brewery spokesmen admit in private) really a pale mild; and an acceptable dark mild (1035). *Charrington's* beers have also been brewed mostly at Cape Hill since the Mile End brewery was closed in 1975; the brews are the sweet but consistent IPA (1039), the thin, bland Crown bitter (1036), which Tolly Cobbold have also brewed for Charrington, and a thin mild (1035). Much more sought-after beers which are only supplied to restricted areas in the West Midlands are Springfield bitter (1036), brewed at Wolverhampton, and Highgate mild (1034), a superb malty dark mild from the Walsall brewery, which has somehow managed to avoid closure.

The *Bass Worthington* brewery at Burton-on-Trent gives some relief to the M & B drinker, amongst others, in the form of draught Bass (1044), a beautiful, distinctive bitter which is one of the few nationally available real beers, and one of the few to have been increased in strength recently. There is also Worthington bitter (1036) and Joule's bitter, now defunct, but in any case described in the CAMRA Good Beer Guide as 'a pale shadow of an old brew'. Worthington's White Shield (1053) is a naturally-conditioned, bottled pale ale. Further north, *Stones* best bitter (1038), an excellent full-bodied bitter from the Sheffield brewery, is widely available in South Yorkshire, and a number of real draught beers, none of them spectacular, is brewed at the *Bass North* plant in Tadcaster. The brews here are Brew Ten (1036), widely available but disappointingly bland, Extra Light Bitter (1033), a mediocre beer which resembles a light mild in palate, and dark mild (1034). Scotland has minute quantities of *Tennent's* 60/– light (1031), a standard light mild. Wales is much better provided for, since *Welsh Brewers* produce HB (1037), which is a pleasant bitter, Hancock's (or Worthington) PA (1033), a light mild, and Worthington dash, or dark mild (1033) at the former Hancock's brewery in Cardiff.

Courage seems to have no real faith in traditional beer, except perhaps in the lucrative south-east. The breweries at Tadcaster and Newark, controlled by their subsidiary John Smith's, produce bright beer only, and the Berkshire Brewery, near Reading, now appears likely to produce bright beer only, so that the excellent brews from the old Simonds brewery in Reading are under sentence of death. The long-term future of the other southern breweries must also be in doubt, since Courage has spare land next to the Berkshire Brewery, which must be ripe for expansion. Undoubtedly Reading produced the outstanding Courage beers – the magnificent, truly bitter and consistent best bitter, and the finest dark mild in southern England. By contrast, the London brews are no more than average: best bitter (1040) lacks a really full taste, though the dark mild (1032) is at best an excellent drink, and Director's bitter (1047), now also brewed at Bristol, is a good strong bitter. The Bristol brewery produces the very bland, weak ordinary bitter (1030) and a sweet, acceptable best bitter (1039). The Stonehouse brewery in Plymouth makes best bitter (1039), a well-hopped and eminently drinkable beer, and heavy (1032), an excellent mild which has been facing withdrawal for years, with the vicious circle of no promotion, restricted availability, and hence declining demand. Courage's London brewery also produces Russian Imperial Stout (1102), a naturally-conditioned bottled beer with a unique flavour.

Guinness is the most widely available naturally-conditioned beer of all: not the so-called 'draught' version, which is all keg, but the bottled beer, a unique and really outstanding dry stout (1042 in summer, 1045 in winter: the brewery claim that this is because of public demand, but who has heard anyone order 'a weak Guinness, please' in a pub?). Dublin-brewed Guinness is the rule in the north of England; further south, Guinness from Park Royal, London, is more common. Connoisseurs prefer the Dublin version, for some obscure reason.

Scottish & Newcastle is in some respects the most intransigent of the Big Six in satisfying demands for real draught beer: Newcastle and much of Scotland suffer most from his attitude. But the Fountain brewery in Edinburgh produces four draught beers, sold under two brand names: *McEwans* 80/– or best Scotch (1043), a very full-flavoured bitter, and 70/– or Scotch (1036), an ordinary bitter; and *Younger's* IPA (1043) and XXPS or Scotch bitter (1036) – the coincidence of original gravities is remarkable. Real beer is available in very few tied houses, and in a minority of free trade outlets, though a few London pubs have real ale again (a few Newcastle pubs could do with it rather more urgently). S & N have gone in for the hard sell with Tartan and Newcastle Exhibition, and real ale is low on their list of priorities; the superb Younger's No. 3 Scotch Ale has been withdrawn in the last few years, and the survivors listed above cannot be completely safe from 'rationalization'.

Watney Mann & Truman Brewers in some respects encapsulate the real ale revival, since from 1975 Watneys, which had all but phased out traditional beer, repented and began to produce one cask beer after another, at least in some parts of the country. But it should be remembered that most of these new real beers are relatively expensive and some of them are less than spectacular. Furthermore, cask-conditioned beer still accounts for a small proportion of Watney's production. *Wilson's*, the Manchester subsidiary, produces the smooth and creamy Great Northern bitter (1037), dark mild (1032) and the newly introduced and insipid Brewer's bitter (1032). Most of Wilson's pubs serve real beer, and new pubs now also tend to get real beer, a welcome change which many other brewers could follow.

Across the Pennines in Halifax, *Samuel Webster* still brews traditional beer for about one in ten of its houses; the beers are Pennine bitter (1037), which is light and fairly sweet, and a full-bodied best mild (1034). *Usher's* of Trowbridge also brews two true draught beers, a remarkable state of affairs since in the early 1970s only the bland PA (1031) remained, best bitter having been withdrawn to allow the brewery to concentrate on production of Watney's national keg and bright beers. Now best bitter (1038), sweet but pleasant, has been revived.

The most curious events in the Watney empire have been taking place at Norwich, where several real beers were brewed for other parts of the country while East Anglia remained in the grip of processed beers until Norwich Castle bitter appeared in 1978. The real beers are Fined Bitter (1044) for London and the East Midlands – an expensive and sweet best bitter – together with Tamplin's bitter (1038) for the south coast, Mann's bitter (1039) for some parts of the Midlands, Norwich Castle bitter (1038) and one or two others. The position in respect of Watney's range of real beers is, to say the least, fluid. Truman's brewery in Brick Lane produces Tap bitter (1039). Pressurized dispense is normal for some of these beers.

Whitbread currently operates fifteen breweries, of which nine, mostly in the south of England, produce real draught beer. The number producing real draught beer has fallen steadily over the years – the breweries at Liverpool and Salford were switched to bright beer production in 1974 (though real ale was reintroduced in 1978) and the Rhymney brewery was closed in 1978 – and there are fears for some of the remaining handful, such as Tiverton and Castle Eden, which could go bright, and Romsey and Cheltenham, which could close altogether. The old Nimmo's brewery at Castle Eden produces Trophy bitter (1041) in real draught form for a handful of outlets. At Cheltenham Trophy is now a bright beer, and the sole surviving real beer is the bland and insipid PA (1031). The former Starkey, Knight & Ford brewery at Tiverton saw the loss of XX mild in 1976, but still brews Trophy (1036) and the very palatable best bitter (1039) – though there are fears that these will be chilled and filtered only before long. At Romsey an excellent mild (1031) and a rather bland Trophy (1038) are offered, but the brewery is so close to the more modern plant at Portsmouth that some rationalization is only to be anticipated.

The Whitbread breweries at Portsmouth, Faversham and Marlow do not, at least in the short term, appear to be under the same kind of threatening cloud (although the development of a fourth Whitbread mega-brewery, somewhere in the south, would threaten all of them). The former *Brickwood's* brewery at Portsmouth produces a lot of real ale, and more than half the pubs supplied from the brewery serve it

– one or more of Pompey Royal (1046), which is the renamed Brickwood's Best, an excellent full-flavoured bitter, the altogether less impressive Trophy (1036), and dark mild (1031). Only a small proportion of Whitbread pubs in Kent offer real draught Trophy (1037) from *Fremlin's* old brewery in Faversham, yet at its best the beer is a really good well-hopped ordinary bitter. Fortunately the reverse, in terms of outlets, is true at the *Thomas Wethered* brewery in Marlow, which has been allowed to retain a surprising amount of individuality. The result is a wide range of excellent draught beers, served traditionally in many of the pubs: a fine dark mild (1031), Trophy bitter (1036: called draught bitter in London, where Trophy is a processed beer from Luton), special bitter (1041), and the full-flavoured Winter Royal (1057).

Postscript

The emergence of new breweries, and also the introduction of new beers by existing brewers, has shown no signs of abating during 1978. New beers from established brewers include Centenary Ale (1050) from Elgood's, a strong dark brew celebrating the firm's hundred years of brewing; Ipswich Special Bitter (1042), test-marketed by Tolly Cobbold; and Randall's Real Ale (1042), a strong bitter produced by Randall's of Jersey (the Guernsey Randall's is a completely separate company) for a CAMRA beer festival, and possibly on a regular basis. New real draught beers from the Big Six include Mann's IPA, yet another real beer from Watney's; Castle Eden Ale, a replacement for Whitbread's Castle Eden Trophy; and Threlfall's bitter, from Whitbread's Liverpool brewery.

Several brand-new brewing enterprises have also entered the fray. Two separate ventures have got under way in Avon: Roger Walkey, a former head brewer at Courage's

Bristol plant, is planning to brew in an old explosives factory at Temple Cloud, and his former colleague at Courage, Simon Whitmore, has set up a brewery a few miles away at Butcombe. The Norfolk House Hotel in Bristol Road, Gloucester, has joined the list of home-brew pubs with Hawthorn's bitter. And Lloyd's Country bitter, available in free houses in part of the East Midlands, is actually brewed at the John Thompson brewery. New licensees, Sidney and Patricia Cannon, have taken over at the Blue Anchor in Helston, Cornwall, although the brewer is still Ted Richards. Yet more new breweries, as far apart as London, Andover and Cumbria, together with further home-brew pubs, are likely to emerge in the near future. One cloud on the horizon, however, is the poor quality control (and, therefore, indifferent beer) of some of the recently established brewers; it is to be hoped that those involved will realize that drinkers want not only a better *choice* of beers but also good *quality* beers.

Further Reading

Frank Baillie, *The Beer Drinker's Companion*, David & Charles, 1973.

Richard Boston, *Beer and Skittles*, Collins, 1976.

Campaign for Real Ale, *The Good Beer Guide*, CAMRA and Arrow Books, annually. CAMRA's monthly newspaper, *What's Brewing*, is also outstandingly informative (subscription rates from 34 Alma Road, St Albans, Herts.).

H. S. Corran, *A History of Brewing*, David & Charles, 1975.

Christopher Hutt, *The Death of the English Pub*, Arrow Books and Hutchinson, 1973.

Michael Jackson, *The World Guide to Beer*, Mitchell Beazley, 1977.

Peter Mathias, *The Brewing Industry in England 1700–1830*, Cambridge University Press, 1959.

H. A. Monckton. *A History of English Ale and Beer*, Bodley Head, 1966.

John Vaizey, *The Brewing Industry 1886–1951: an Economic Study*, Pitman, 1960.

Index

More About Penguins and Pelicans

Penguinews, which appears every month, contains details of all the new books issued by Penguins as they are published. From time to time it is supplemented by our stocklist, which includes around 5,000 titles.

A specimen copy of *Penguinews* will be sent to you free on request. Please write to Dept EP, Penguin Books Ltd, Harmondsworth, Middlesex, for your copy.

In the U.S.A.: For a complete list of books available from Penguins in the United States write to Dept CS, Penguin Books, 625 Madison Avenue, New York, New York 10022.

In Canada: For a complete list of books available from Penguins in Canada write to Penguin Books Canada Ltd, 2801 John Street, Markham, Ontario L3R 1B4.

Penguin Handbooks

Penguin Handbooks offer an enormous range of useful guides to help you with cooking, drinking, sewing, knitting gardening, sports, hobbies, child care, the law – all these and many more. Some of them are listed on the following pages.

Cookery and wine

The Farmhouse Kitchen

Mary Norwak

A bevy of recipes, with notes on their history, which includes all the traditional country occupations of bread-making, pickling and brewing, as well as delicious and time-honoured meals.

Vegetable Cookery

Nika Hazelton

An A-Z of vegetables, both fresh and dried, with their history, ways of keeping and preserving them, their nutritional value, and a host of exciting recipes.

Leave It To Cook

Stella Attenbury

Slow cooking makes food taste better and saves time. Here are recipes for meat, fish, soups, casseroles, vegetables, sweets and savouries that you can leave for up to eight hours and only improve the taste.

Herbs For All Seasons

Rosemary Hemphill

In four parts, one for each season, this book gives instructions for planting, growing and drying each plant, with a variety of recipes to suit all tastes and a fascinating collection of herbal remedies and beauty aids.

A Taste of the Country

Pamela Westland

An ardent advocate of home produce, Pamela Westland gives a list of the crops you can grow in your garden and recipes for dealing with them.

English Food

Jane Grigson

'Jane Grigson is perhaps the most serious and discriminating of the younger generation of cookery writers, and *English Food* is an anthology all who follow her recipes will want to buy' – Pamela Vandyke Price in the *Spectator*

The Penguin Book of Jams, Pickles and Chutneys

David and Rose Mabey

'An excellent book; practical, personal and suggestive, every recipe's clearly the result of real experience and written with great charm' – *The Times*

Cooking with Wine

Robin McDouall

You'd be surprised at the number of delicious ways you can disguise Calvados, sherry, Champagne, beer, cider – and, of course, wine . . .

The Penguin Book of Home Brewing and Wine-Making

W. H. T. Tayleur

Here is all you need to know about beer and wine, liqueurs and cider, perry and mead; how to make them, bottle them, store them and serve them. You'll know how to drink them!

A Wine Primer

André Simon

André Simon guides us gently along the great galleries of the Aperitifs, the famous Beverage wines, and the Dessert wines, concluding with a sparkling review of wines for special occasions.